LIVING WITH LIFE'S LIMPS

It is not that you limp that matters...
It is how you limp that matters!

Dr. Dwayne Pickett

LIVING WITH LIFE'S LIMPS

Dr. Dwayne Pickett

Copyright 2017.

Printed in the United States of America.

All Rights Reserved.

The testimonies in chapters eight through eleven are true stemming from live interviews with the author. However, some of the names have been changed at the requests of those interviewed.

No part of this work may be reproduced or transmitted in any form or by any means, electronic or mechanical, including photocopying and recording, or by any information storage or retrieval system, except as may be expressly permitted by the 1976 Copyright Act or in writing from the publisher.

ISBN: 978-0-9974318-2-7

CONTENTS

1. Limping — 9
2. Limping for God's Glory — 21
3. The Limper's Life: Life Realities — 33
4. Jacob Limped — 43
5. Mephibosheth Limped — 51
6. Jesus Identifies With Our Limps — 63
7. Social Limps — 73
8. Emotional Limps — 93
9. Sexual Limps — 103
10. Mental Limps — 127
11. Physical Limps — 147

Epilogue — 159

LIVING WITH LIFE'S LIMPS *was not written as another self-help book. But as you read each page, you will discover essential keys that will help unlock the door to a better you—not a perfect you. In this book, Dr. Dwayne Pickett shares his personal experiences, practical wisdom, and biblical principles. By applying these principles, readers will discover hidden treasures within. God made us all uniquely different on purpose, and when we accept the glaring reality that we all have flaws and issues, this truth will set us free. I am convinced that when we confront and deal with the issues that hinder us in life and make the necessary changes, we will experience total prosperity. I applaud Dr. Pickett for his courage and transparency in writing this great book.*

    Bishop Paul S. Morton, Sr.
    Founder, Full Gospel Baptist Church Fellowship International
    Senior Pastor, Changing a Generation Ministries, Atlanta, Georgia
    Overseer and Co-Pastor, Greater St. Stephen Ministries,
    New Orleans, Louisiana

If you're headed into a new adventure, it's vital to talk to someone who has been there before. Dwayne Pickett has been there. He's been to hell and back. He's faced adversity, death, and disappointment, and he's won the victory. In LIVING WITH LIFE'S LIMPS, *he gives us the pathway to freedom, success, and fulfillment. I thank God for a man like Dr. Pickett who will be real—not give us a cute little formula but the real stuff of life—and tell us how to live strong. Never learn from a man who walks without a limp. The man who limps is the true champion.*

    Paul Louis Cole
    President, Christian Men's Network Global

One of the great joys of my life is to know and to work with Dwayne Pickett. He is a leader. He is an innovator. He is a family man. And he is a man of God. Even more, he has an incredible story, a story that will inspire, motivate, and change your life. But his book, LIVING WITH LIFE'S LIMPS, *is not just his story; it is our story as well. Read it. Apply it. And live it.*

    Thom S. Rainer
    President and CEO, LifeWay Christian Resources

LIVING WITH LIFE'S LIMPS *is a book saturated in authenticity and transparency. Its honesty is encouraging. My friend, Dwayne Pickett, teaches an inspiring lesson. He helps unpack the conundrum of the duplicitous Jacob/Israel nature that lies within humanity. You'll be encouraged to know that God still uses flawed people, despite their imperfections.*

    Bishop Dale Carnegie Bronner
    Founder and Senior Pastor, Word of Faith Family Worship Cathedral
    Atlanta, Georgia

Acknowledgements

I want to dedicate this book to my wife who has walked with me with my limps. She stood by my side through some of the toughest moments of my life. She wrote me two letters a day while I was deployed overseas fighting for our country, she bathed me when I could not bathe myself after my life changing accident, and she has stayed married to a limper for over 25 years. I want to thank my amazing wife, friend, and ministry partner who has worked tirelessly to get this book completed.

FOREWORD

I sat in the passenger seat of my big brother's truck. I don't know why he thought I was worthy of hearing his testimony, but it poured out of him anyway. I live thousands of miles away. I hadn't heard much about what had happened to him or why it nearly brought tears to his eyes to tell me.

But when he told it, it almost brought tears to my eyes.

We don't think these things can happen to a preacher. They're supermen. They are supposed to hit the ground and get right back up unscathed. That's not my brother's testimony, though. His tragedy left a mark. It left a limp. It left a hitch in his walk that anyone could see. But more spectacular than the new injury was the old motor that kept him going. It kept him preaching four services at three locations every Sunday, traveling through the week, and running businesses. That motor kept him trusting God and serving God's people.

I was inspired. Call it the Holy Spirit or my God-made, strange mind, but as he told me the details of his impending recovery—the stitches, the rehab, the surgery, and the scars—I remembered all the weird turns my life had taken, the emotional accidents and intellectual crashes that I'd endured. I remembered the scars that still blemish my thinking, my esteem, and my ability to love. They ultimately make it harder and more complicated to trust God and pursue this faith. Oh, but for the grace that allows us to grab victory from the jaws of defeat. It's a victory that doesn't come from losing the limp, but it comes from choosing never to stop walking.

Thank God for that big brother in the faith, Pastor Pickett. Limps were supposed to stop his ministry. Turns out, they *are* his ministry.

>Jonathan McReynolds
>National Recording Artist

1. LIMPING

"The sun rose above [Jacob] as he passed Peniel, and he was limping because of his hip."
(Genesis 32:31, emphasis added)

I have limped for a long time, but I didn't know it until one Sunday morning in December 2006. I was on my way to Voices of Faith Ministries outside Atlanta, Georgia, to preach the second service when a minivan crashed head-on into the car I was riding in. This accident proved to be a pivotal moment in my life.

Before the accident, I thought I was living fully in the will of God. I didn't know that my past sin and rebellion and the pain inflicted on me by others I trusted had impacted me negatively in many ways. I was actually stumbling through life because of my past sin and rebellion, as well as from the pain inflicted on me by others I trusted.

Although it appeared that everything was good on the outside, I was limping on the inside. After my physical injuries forced me to limp on the outside, on the inside, I was finally learning how much more I had to learn about walking with Jesus.

I had to be afflicted with a real, physical limp to understand the life-changing message God wanted to give me. But before I tell you how that happened, I want to tell you about myself so you can see that I am no different than you are. If God has used someone like me, despite me and my circumstances, then He can and will use you, too.

Just When It Was All Coming Together

Before the car accident, God was growing and expanding my ministry as the pastor of a congregation that had grown from 180 members to 6,000 members. People were coming into saving, life-giving relationships with God. However, such "success" can be dangerous for pastors because everyone pats them on the back and gives them all the credit.

A lot of people seemed to think that I was something. I was invited to speak at churches and major events around the world, and things were moving to a high level. So it seemed totally illogical for God to shut me down, but God's ways are not our ways: "How unsearchable are his judgments, and his ways past finding out!" (Romans 11:33, KJV).

> IF GOD HAS USED SOMEONE LIKE ME, DESPITE ME AND MY CIRCUMSTANCES, THEN HE CAN AND WILL USE YOU, TOO.

Then I found myself being cut out of a car by emergency responders with the Jaws of Life. It took over seven surgeries to put my body back together. The right side of my face was totally reconstructed. Metal was inserted up and down the right side of my body and my face.

Today, I still have metal in my right leg and in the right side of my face. Doctors told me that due to the accident, one of my legs would be shorter than the other and I would probably walk with a limp for the rest of my life.

I could not believe that I might be physically limping for the rest of my life. Life can be cruel, and I had to face this new reality. For a while, though, I tried to mask the limp as best as I could, so I got shoe inserts so it wouldn't be as noticeable. I tried to fool myself and others into thinking that I did not have a limp. I thought that maybe I could make it look like I was "pimping" instead of limping (pimping as in an animated walk from the 1970s).

All of my life, I had tried to hide behind things and to have my own way. I wanted God to use me, but I realize in hindsight how my limp needed to happen in order for Him to use me for His glory.

My relationship with God started in childhood. I was born and raised in Itta Bena, Mississippi, by way of Terry, Mississippi. The prejudice that I have experienced throughout my life could have easily made me bitter and angry, but the love of God caused me to forgive.

Though my father and mother were professors at nearby Mississippi Valley State University, my family's life outside of academia was typical of most blacks in that area. In the 1980s, I lived the same life as the men I admired while growing up. I partied through my high school and early college years, but I still sat in church from time to time. I was strangely drawn to what I now know was Christ's saving Spirit.

I was surprised when God called me to preach in March 1990. If I wrote down my sin history, it would fill volumes. But God took this guy, who had been living a horrible, sinful life, and collided him into His grace. I used to think God kept a scorecard, and at the end of your life, if you did more good than bad, you were accepted. But one Sunday morning, I ran into God's grace, and He spoke clearly to me.

But after meeting God's grace, I went out that Sunday night, and I did what I always did—partying and reveling. That Monday morning, however, something was different. I woke up with a restlessness on the inside, not knowing where it came from.

I ran to the front of the house to get my mother's car keys so I could drive to my grandmother's house and talk to her. I thought she could help me understand what I was going through. My mother did not let me use the car, so I ran back to my room and locked the door. I fell on my face and said, "If there is a God in heaven, I need to know!" At that moment, my mother somehow opened that locked door and fell on her knees beside me.

I know now that it was the Holy Spirit. My mother led me in prayer to receive Christ. I stood up and played "Thank You for All You've Done" by the Jackson Southernaires. (I don't know how that record got on my record player.) When I looked outside, everything literally looked brand-new. Even though it may be cliché to say so, but my hands and feet looked new, too. I knew that God had touched me.

> I ASKED GOD, "WHAT DO YOU WANT FROM ME?" GOD ANSWERED CLEARLY: "TO PREACH THE WORD."

A month later, I was driving down Highway 59, headed to see my son Julian. As I was driving, I asked God, "What do you want from me?" God answered clearly: "To preach the Word."

Soon after hearing from God, I was preparing to preach my first sermon. Around the same time, I learned that I was going to have another son by another woman. I found out when she was seven months pregnant. I was shocked. It seemed as if my past had come back to haunt me.

I asked God, "How could you let this happen to me?" My question was self-centered because I could not see my own fault in all of this. Promiscuity had been sown deep inside of me by men in my life, but I offer no excuses today.

"God," I asked, "how could you let my past come back to haunt me?" I was so naïve. I didn't understand sin's consequences. I was just in utter despair. I went to church that next Sunday, but I felt like all eyes were on me, so I ran out. Again, I fled back into the world. I was running away from God. I was bitter and confused, so I went back to what I knew.

In September, I found myself in Riyadh, Saudi Arabia, in Desert Storm with the 162nd MP Company, 112th military battalion. Tracy, my wife-to-be and the mother of my first son, Julian, wrote me letters while I was there. During mail call, I always received two or three letters from her. Out of all of the relationships I had been involved in with women, she stood by me during my most challenging time. As a matter of fact, she is still doing the same thing today.

I proposed to Tracy from overseas, and we married in May 1991 after I returned to Mississippi. But I was still running from God. It's a wonder He didn't just let me go, but His grace is so amazing! I had promised the Lord that if He brought me back from Saudi Arabia, I would preach His Word. Meanwhile, I almost died three times, caught up in the craziness of that same carousing lifestyle.

Still, I was attending church. One night, while stationed at Fort Benning, Georgia, I went to church with a godly elderly woman in the woods of Alabama. A pastor named Larry B. Aiken preached a sermon entitled "If I Knew Then What I Know Right Now."

After tears and prayers, I called my pastor to tell him that I had to obey God. A couple of weeks later, I preached my first sermon at Christian Unity Church in Laurel, Mississippi, and later joined Mt. Olive Baptist Church in Hattiesburg. After graduating from Southern Miss with my master's degree, I enrolled at Reformed Theological Seminary in Jackson.

My father, Pick, often spoke at black churches to help them get a vision for educational opportunities for their youth. By this time, he was high up in the state's department of education. He would also become its first black commissioner of education, serving on an interim basis. I attended one small church event with him. That church, New Jerusalem Missionary Baptist Church, later invited me back to preach. But their invitation was out of appreciation to my father.

In a matter of months, New Jerusalem asked me to become their interim pastor. I was not expecting or desiring this position at all. What happened late in 1995 was totally of God and by His grace. In just a few years, this inner-city church of 180 members grew to more than 6,000 and now has over 8,000 members.

Today, New Jerusalem is one church with four locations throughout the Jackson area, and we conduct four Sunday services. God has been good to allow me to complete a PhD from New Orleans Baptist Seminary, becoming the third African American person to receive a doctorate in the seminary's Christian education department.

Has this all been smooth sailing? No, nothing is ever smooth in God's great work. Opposition comes from Satan, from the world, and from the flesh. Others let me down, and I've let others down. You will read some of those stories and what I've learned from them.

A former alcoholic, dope-smoking, womanizing, partying, no-good, egg-sucking dog with two children out of wedlock by two different women is not even supposed to be alive. But God's work has continued for God's glory and no one else's.

The Lesson of the Limp

How can God take a brazen sinner and use him to touch thousands in Mississippi and beyond? Let me tell you how: He taught me the lesson of walking with limps.

God used a car crash to reveal this life-changing truth to me. Through my physical limp, I finally saw that I had been limping all along. I had been fraught with spiritual, emotional, and physical issues that were causing me to limp through life. The tremendous biblical metaphor of limping, which seems to run from the start to the end of Scripture, began to help me make sense of my life in a whole new way.

Walking with limps is like going through divine physical therapy that lasts your whole life. It is a process. It is repetitive. It is grueling. It can be frustrating. It can be humbling. However, if you understand the plan and the goals, it works because it is Gospel-driven.

> WALKING WITH LIMPS IS LIKE GOING THROUGH DIVINE PHYSICAL THERAPY THAT LASTS YOUR WHOLE LIFE.

In my recovery after the car accident, I visited a physical therapist. If I got out of order with my therapy, my therapist corrected me. To regain my ability to walk, I had to do painstaking tasks in just the right order and sequence for the plan to work.

It helped me in my recovery when I understood why the therapist wanted to do a certain exercise in a certain way. It helped me when my therapist told me what I could expect along my road to recovery. Knowing the plan made limping a lot easier to endure.

God graciously has already healed the physical limp (which is an absolute miracle as it resulted from a second surgery on the same leg due to a re-injury) as well as the severe pain, and I am trusting Him to take away all of my pain in His own time. More importantly, He also used my injury and that limp to reveal to me that we have deeper limps.

We may try to hide them from others and even from ourselves, but they are still there. In the honesty of our hearts, we know that we're crippled and we need to work on these limps with God's help and guidance. God's divine therapy works.

I limp for God's glory because Jesus has been as merciful to me as He was to some of those who were physically lame in the New Testament. I was like them—another of those many men on a mat, crying out and begging for help.

Don't let this next statement cause you to put down this book because it doesn't line up with your theology: I believe that we all limp in some fashion as long as we are being conformed into the image of Christ. In other words, until Jesus returns, we have to deal with this fallen world and totally depend on the Holy Spirit to lead us through this life.

Limps are those realities in life that can set us back and hold us up. They are those areas of life—physically, emotionally, and spiritually—that can cripple us. The good news is that if we turn to God, He will use our limps to form character and Christlikeness in us. Then we start walking with limps for God's glory.

In what area do you have a limp that might be holding you back in life? What is crippling you? Do you want to have a deeper walk with Jesus?

The concept of limping is a powerful one in the Scriptures, so let's look into what the Bible teaches about the crippled and limping outcasts that Jesus loved so much. I invite you to consider how your life could change if you were free to admit that you limp and could learn to overcome your limps God's way for God's purposes.

If you will come with me on this journey, I will encourage you to adopt your own divine spiritual therapy plan to get you up on your feet and to overcome limps. It won't always be easy, but God will get all of the glory, and you and others will receive the blessings.

2. LIMPING FOR GOD'S GLORY

"For from him and through him and to him are all things. To him be the glory forever! Amen." (Romans 11:36)

I am so grateful that God loves those of us who limp, those of us the world has counted out (1 Corinthians 1:27). When He was here on earth, Jesus sought out the lost, those who had been crippled and maimed by life and by their own sinfulness (Luke 19:10).

Today, our Savior still seeks people like that, like us, because He loves us anyway (Romans 5:8). That's why everything I want to say to you starts with this statement: God's goal is for you to limp for His glory, so overcome your limp—no matter what that might be—for His glory. That might sound strange to you, but Jesus' mission definitely goes against the norms of society, which often reject the outcasts.

The Bible shows that those who limped or were impaired were cast out and desperate. Such people knew that they were imperfect and in need of help. The good news is that God the Father sent Jesus, His Son, who seeks not only to help us but also to save us and give us abundant life (John 10:10). God wants to use us, fellowship with us, and know us, even with our imperfections.

So, our imperfections do not negate God's plan for our lives. Although we may be walking with limps or we may be lame, we can still experience a fulfilling life by trusting fully in Jesus. Living life through Christ helps us to overcome the realities of our limps.

It is not that you limp that matters. It is how you limp that matters.

> BEING HEALED DOES NOT ALWAYS LOOK LIKE PERFECTION. SOMETIMES THERE MAY BE SCARS OF SOME KIND THAT MARK WHERE WE WERE ONCE IMPAIRED OR WOUNDED.

Healing Agents: Love and Grace

Life hits us with pain, sin, and failure, and the Bible often uses the metaphor of us being crippled by such realities. We all were born disabled. Our humanity, the fact that we are born in sin and shaped in iniquity, constitutes a limp of overwhelming proportions that would maim us for life if we didn't have the Lord's help.

I'm not promising that if you read this book you will live a limp-free life, because Jesus didn't promise that either. That would almost be like promising you a trouble-free life. This book talks about how to glorify God while walking with the limps that life's tribulations, the world, our own flesh, and the devil have inflicted on us.

As you read this book, I hope you will see two life-giving, encouraging things about Jesus' relationship with those who limp. First, God holds His deepest love for us. Why? Because we are broken and in need of help. God hears our cries of desperation and distress. God's promise to us is that those who take His hand will one day be fully restored. "The lame [will] leap like a deer" (Isaiah 35:6). God says, "I will gather the lame" (Micah 4:6); and "when you give a banquet, invite . . . the lame" (Luke 14:13).

God provides the healing and the strength we need, even if it is sometimes through a difficult process. Hebrews 12:11-13 says, "No discipline seems pleasant at the time, but painful. Later on, however, it produces a harvest of righteousness and peace for those who have been trained by it. Therefore, strengthen your feeble arms and weak knees. 'Make level paths for your feet,' so that the lame may not be disabled, but rather healed."

Being healed does not always look like perfection. Sometimes there may be scars of some kind that mark where we were once impaired or wounded.

Consider this example: When a person breaks an ankle, the doctor puts screws in the broken bone. That person then goes through physical therapy. The patient progresses from experiencing total pain that permits no weight on the ankle, to hobbling with pain, to walking with a slight limp, and then to walking with no apparent limp at all. But X-rays often still show an imperfect or incomplete alignment of the bones. Is this person healed? Yes.

Second, God tells us that we can make it together by His grace. He encourages those who are lame to limp right back out into the world and love others who are limping—which is everyone! Hebrews 12:14-15 helps those who limp know how to live among others: "Make *every effort* to live in peace with everyone and to be holy; without holiness no one will see the Lord. See to it that no one falls short of the grace of God and that no bitter root grows up to cause trouble and defile many" (emphasis added).

Jesus Knows and Understands

It may be hard to believe right now, especially if you are wounded or in pain, but a limp-free life does not bring you real joy because a limp-free life is one devoid of Jesus. Rather, it is the realities of our limps that cause us to lean on Jesus, and that offers us true joy. God enters in, and we are enriched and enabled. The good news is that we "can do all things through Christ" (Philippians 4:13, NKJV), even walk with limps.

Who is this Christ? The Bible says that Jesus "*made himself nothing* by taking the very nature of *a servant*, being made in human likeness. And being found in appearance as a man, he *humbled* himself" (Philippians 2:7-8, emphasis added). The Bible says that Jesus was despised and rejected by men, which means Jesus humbled Himself and made Himself despised like one of us.

Jesus surely understood the hopeless people around Him, crippled by sin—their own and others. But more than that, Jesus understood from Scripture that there were spiritual, moral, and emotional constraints on the lame. So, God's heart went out to them as He demonstrated His love by sending His Son to redeem them.

Jesus was not overcome by the limps of life. He was sinless, resisting the temptations of the enemy. In His humility and obedience, He subjected Himself to our frailties and faced trials and tribulations as we do. He became our example of how through Him it is possible to live in victory despite the circumstances of life that maim us or cause us to limp.

> A LIMP-FREE LIFE DOES NOT BRING YOU REAL JOY BECAUSE A LIMP-FREE LIFE IS ONE DEVOID OF JESUS.

Satan constantly attacked Jesus. People hated and persecuted Him, and good friends rejected Him. He grew weary, and He wept and felt emotional pain. He felt frustration, anger, and deep sadness. He felt overwhelmed. When Jesus became a man, He identified with our weaknesses and our deficiencies firsthand, and He didn't promise us that we would face anything different.

The apostle John said, "Whoever claims to live in [Christ] must live as Jesus did" (1 John 2:6). How did Jesus live? Jesus told us to deny ourselves, take up our cross daily, and follow him (Luke 9:23).

Jesus bore the burden of our limps as He carried the cross to Golgotha. On the cross, Christ went beyond facing the pain and suffering of a hard life and was laden beyond our imagination by our sins. So Jesus escaped nothing. On His pilgrimage to the cross, He felt pain and suffered injustice and verbal persecution. He experienced the full consequence of our sin. Jesus endured the weight of our limps on the cross as He laid down His life on our behalf.

But then Jesus added, "But take heart! I have overcome the world" (John 16:33). Jesus said that the way to peace is to understand that your life will not be trouble-free; you will limp in this world. But just

> JUST AS JESUS OVERCAME THE WORLD, HE HELPS US TO DO THE SAME. BY HIS POWER WE HAVE HOPE.

as He overcame the world, He helps us to do the same. By His power we have hope.

Limps Defined

In the Bible, the word *walk* implies steady wholeness, while the word *limp* implies unsteady brokenness. It's the same today. A standard dictionary definition of each word reveals the difference. *To walk* is "to advance on foot at a moderate speed or pace in a steady, even way." *To limp* is "to walk with a labored, jerky movement, as when lame." Metaphorically, which better describes how you live your life: smooth and efficient or jerky and inefficient?

The reason we limp might be to humble us, to keep us humble, or to ensure our humility. Of course, Satan relishes the fact that we limp, and he tries to use it to his advantage to bring about our demise because he wants to thwart Jesus' work in our lives.

When it comes to limping, we tend to fall into one of three categories. The first two are bad, and it is Satan's goal to keep you stuck in one of these two mindsets. But the third one is good, and my goal in writing this book is to point you in that direction.

Wallowing. Satan prefers this condition since it causes people to remain in self-pity. Christians and non-Christians alike who wallow think everyone should pity them because of past pains, sins, or failures that have caused physical, emotional, or spiritual suffering.

Christians who wallow might appear to be trying hard to follow Jesus, but they are just dwelling on their impairments. Somewhere along the line, they stopped living in God's power and started living in self-pity. When their limps showed up, instead of going the way of Christ-like humility, they went the way of self-centered anger and pity.

If you are like this, I pray that you will begin walking victoriously with your limps as God reveals to you His powerful mercy. The Bible says, " 'Even now . . . return to me with all your heart.' . . . For [I am] gracious and compassionate, slow to anger and abounding in love. . . . Who knows? [I] may turn and relent and leave behind a blessing" (Joel 2:12-14).

The Bible warns us about wallowing in our limps. "The way of the sluggard is blocked with thorns, but the path of the upright is a highway" (Proverbs 15:19). You are meant to hit the road for Jesus. Get on the highway! You may be limping, but God will make your life a highway to limp on rather than a byway toward pity. The sluggard gets caught up in thorns on the byway and never makes progress. Such a life is lazy living "blocked with thorns."

"I don't have it in me," someone says. "I'm just waiting on heaven." This person may sound humble, but that attitude isn't humble; it's hopeless.

God asks, "How long will you lie there, you sluggard?" (Proverbs 6:9). How long will you lie there with your limp? God calls us to a life of walking with limps, which means overcoming our limps and our insecurities for His glory.

Faking, Stroking, Denying. People who are faking, stroking, or denying are trying to hide their limps, pretending they have it all together. They fear facing their inadequacies, pains, and sin. Somewhere pride is lurking.

If this is you, acknowledging your limp dispels your pride before God. Trying to conceal your limp breeds more problems, which may actually be self-inflicted. The Bible says, "In his pride the wicked does not seek [God]; in all of his thoughts there is no room for God" (Psalm 10:4). God says that if you want to walk with Him, you need to remove pride from your life: "I hate pride and arrogance" (Proverbs 8:13).

> YOU ARE MEANT TO HIT THE ROAD FOR JESUS. YOU MAY BE LIMPING, BUT GOD WILL MAKE YOUR LIFE A HIGHWAY TO LIMP ON RATHER THAN A BYWAY TOWARD PITY.

Pride always takes you down, not up. If you are in denial of your condition, then you are setting yourself up for more pain. "Pride goes before destruction, a haughty spirit before a fall" (Proverbs 16:18). This book isn't about helping you fall. Falls only lead to more limps. Face your realities and begin to overcome.

Walking With Limps. Overcoming Limps. Walking with limps or overcoming them means not being impaired by them. Even with the pains and trials of life, humbly trust God (leaning on His grace) to enable you to press forward. "God opposes the proud but gives grace to the humble" (James 4:6, ESV).

Many great people in the Bible started off in pride but finally humbled themselves before God and submitted to His divine plan. Then they received grace, blessing, purpose, and fortitude to glorify God. Despite their inadequacies or weaknesses, they walked in God's strength. This teaches us that when we are weak, then He is strong.

Acknowledge Your Limp

If you hurt your leg, you will probably have a limp. If you ignore that limp, it will get worse, so you need to have it checked out. It is the same with us spiritually. Pain, sin, and failures injure us and cause us to limp. Sometimes we wallow in our limps or try to camouflage them, avoiding God's healing for fear of exposure, but the limps get worse.

We must seek treatment to overcome our limps, and that's why I wrote this book. Are you tired of wanting to serve God one day and then going your own way the next? Then don't wallow or pretend any longer.

I know that you face many challenges, some of which are life-altering, because I have done so, too. Seek God humbly.

Admit the realities of how you limp, and work to overcome them rather than merely work on them.

With prayer and guidance, you can overcome. Soon you will be walking with your limps, holding fast to Jesus. And that's the source of fulfilling God's purpose through your life.

3. THE LIMPER'S LIFE: LIFE REALITIES

"For the Son of Man came to seek and to save the lost." (Luke 19:10)

While on earth, Jesus didn't spend time with the elite. Instead, He sought "the least of these"—the outcasts—such as publicans, tax collectors, and others who were despised by society. Jesus came to the world on a mission to find and empower "the low down and the no good" and to give hope to the lost.

Jesus came to heal and to restore, to give us the power to walk for and with Him. I'm grateful that He came for the sick and not the well (Matthew 9:12), and we should follow His example in our own ministries (Matthew 25:36).

Jesus used every opportunity to reveal His plan of action regarding mankind's sinful limping conditions. It was evident to all He encountered and to all who heard about Him that a major paradigm shift was at hand. Something was changing, not according to man's ways but according to God's ways.

The Real Limp

One of the most amazing limping encounters in the Bible is described in Mark 2. Many people came to hear Jesus' unorthodox teaching. On this occasion, as He was teaching to a packed house, a group of men broke through the roof of the house and lowered the bed of their paralyzed friend in front of Jesus.

> JESUS SAW PEOPLE WHO WOULD GIVE IN AND THOSE WHO COULD BARELY HANG ON, AND HE WANTED TO GIVE US SOMETHING MORE THAN PHYSICAL HEALING.

The man sought physical healing, but Jesus had much more planned for him and would use this episode to convey a larger spiritual reality. When the man descended into the room on his bed, it was as if the curtain of Jesus' entire ministry was drawn open.

Instead of rushing to heal the man's physical ailment, Jesus focused on his spiritual and emotional reality and told the man that his sins were forgiven. The people gathered there were shocked, because when Jesus forgives sin, it is a supernatural and a counter-cultural action. However, I don't believe the man was shocked at all. More than likely, he had never felt so relieved. In addressing all of the man's impairments, Jesus had set him free.

When Jesus saw the man on his bed, I imagine that He also saw everyone He had come to save, including you and me. He saw people who would give in and those who could barely hang on, and He wanted to give us something more than physical healing.

"Why does this fellow talk like that?" asked the teachers in the crowd. "Who can forgive sins but God alone?" They wondered what authority Jesus had that enabled him to forgive sin. They also wanted to know why Jesus would forgive the man's sins when he had initially asked for physical healing.

Jesus, capturing the moment, asked, "Which is easier: to say to this paralyzed man, 'Your sins are forgiven,' or to say, 'Get up, take your mat and walk'?" Then He healed the man's physical impairment as well as his spiritual impairment, revealing His authority to heal any limping condition (Mark 2:6-12).

Jesus' divine therapy plan was now clearly revealed, and it is still effective today. He tied the reality of earth to the reality of heaven by demonstrating a physical miracle as well as a greater spiritual miracle, one that we all need because all of us limp or are impaired in some way.

The Bible says that the crowd was amazed and praised God. While they did not understand the man's spiritual healing, they understood his physical relief. Despite being critical of what had taken place, maybe they also sensed that a new way of looking at life had come into being through Jesus.

The Tax Collector

Jesus had another pivotal encounter, this time with a tax collector named Matthew (Matthew 9). When Matthew decided to follow Jesus, he became the second man in this chapter who "got up." Like the paralytic man, Matthew got up from his mat, too, but it was a spiritual mat. There would soon be thousands of others who would rise from their "mats," too, and today that number is like the sands on the seashore.

When Jesus ate dinner at Matthew's house, He joined His disciples, tax collectors, and other sinners. Jesus' actions again raised questions among the skeptical. How could a religious teacher do such a thing? Tax collectors were hated and despised, but Jesus was about to flip the situation on its head. He entered the house of a presumed sinner of sinners and ate with him. The religious elite had never heard of such a thing.

In his new disciple Matthew, Jesus saw us. Perhaps Matthew's limps included jealousy, envy, greed, and contempt for others, just to name a few. His fellow Jews hated men like him and other people they deemed to be sinners.

Tax collectors, especially, were reviled and treated as outcasts, so Matthew began his spiritual walk with an assortment of emotional and spiritual limps. But Jesus saw in him another "man on a mat," just like the paralytic man He had healed before. He saw someone with emotional, physical, and spiritual limps.

Jesus made a connection with the man on the mat and the tax collector because he was linking physical limps with the root of mankind's primary spiritual limps. He invited two men cast out by society for different reasons to rise and to overcome their limps for His glory. He gave them a new beginning and a new outlook on life despite their imperfections and gave them a sense of hope and purpose. They became members of Jesus' army of believers who, despite their weaknesses and imperfections, had been redeemed and restored through Christ.

> JESUS' PLAN OF VICTORY OVER SIN AND EVIL WAS A PLAN OF LOVING ALL PEOPLE, NO MATTER THEIR CONDITION; AND HE CAME TO SAVE PEOPLE DESPITE THEIR GREATEST LIMPING IMPAIRMENT: SIN.

Jesus came to seek and to save the lost (Luke 19:10), and His entry into the world set His mission in motion. He came to call sinners, not the righteous (Matthew 9:12-13). Jesus' plan of victory over sin and evil was a plan of loving all people, no matter their condition; and He came to save people despite their greatest limping impairment: sin.

Jesus came to earth because He is building a body through which He is establishing His kingdom. So, despite our imperfections, through Christ, we become His instruments as we learn to walk with our limps and do what He has called us to do.

Lifelong Limps

Like the paralyzed man and the tax collector, at some point, all of us have found ourselves on a mat of despair due to our spiritual, physical, and emotional deficiencies. Now it's time for us to get up and start walking with limps and to overcome the realities of our imperfections.

When we do rise and walk, there will be people who may not understand or approve of our healing, just as those people disagreed with Jesus' healing of the paralyzed man and His association with Matthew. What the onlookers couldn't comprehend, they ridiculed. Don't let what others think stop you from reaching your hand out to Jesus. He loves us and meets us where we are.

> ALL OF US HAVE FOUND OURSELVES ON A MAT OF DESPAIR DUE TO OUR SPIRITUAL, PHYSICAL, AND EMOTIONAL DEFICIENCIES. NOW IT'S TIME FOR US TO GET UP AND START WALKING WITH LIMPS AND TO OVERCOME THE REALITIES OF OUR IMPERFECTIONS.

He alone can turn around any situation for our good and for His glory.

Paul

What happens if a limp persists even after we pray for God to remove it? Paul was plagued with a thorn in his flesh, and he prayed earnestly three times for God to remove it. Instead, the Lord told him, "My grace is sufficient for you, for my power is made perfect in weakness" (2 Corinthians 12:9). The Lord is our hope, even with the reality of life's impairments.

Having received this answer, Paul declared that he would rather boast in his infirmities so that the power of Christ might rest on him. He also said, "I delight in weaknesses, in insults, in hardships, in persecutions, in difficulties. For when I am weak, then I am strong" (2 Corinthians 12:10).

The Lord gave Paul hope and assurance that no matter what he faced and endured, God could use him. And Paul was used for God's glory as he wrote much of the New Testament while facing the limps of infirmities, insults, hardships, persecutions, and difficulties. He even acknowledged the necessity of the thorn in his flesh, which he said was "in order to keep [him] from becoming conceited" (2 Corinthians 12:7).

Paul's limp was humbling, but he accepted it with the right attitude in response to God's answer to his prayers. He didn't wallow in his condition. Instead, he forged ahead by God's grace and in His power.

What keeps you on your knees? Paul called his thorn "a messenger of Satan, to torment [him]" (2 Corinthians 12:7). He didn't just have a thorn in his flesh; he was tormented by it. So, we can deduce that Satan was involved in trying to impair or inhibit Paul, and Satan is involved in trying to do the same to us.

> SOMETIMES THE LORD ALLOWS THINGS TO HAPPEN TO ME TO DISCIPLINE AND TO HUMBLE ME. BUT MOST IMPORTANTLY, GOD ALLOWS LIMPS IN MY LIFE SO THAT I WILL LEAN ON HIM AND FOLLOW HIM FAITHFULLY.

Are there things that torment you? Are there times when God allows evil to spring up around you or against you so that you will be disciplined and come to lean on Him instead of other people or things? Sometimes the Lord allows things to happen to me to discipline and to humble me. But most importantly, God allows limps in my life so that I will lean on him and follow Him faithfully.

Paul knew his limp—that source of his pain and problems—but he doesn't tell us exactly what it was. New Testament scholars point to many possibilities. Among them are the areas of emotions, sin and temptation, unbelief, dreams, accidents and incidents, relationships, illness and imperfection, and persecution. While this is not an all-encompassing list of possible limp areas that we might face, it gives us a reasonable number of possibilities to reflect on. All of these areas in some way did affect Paul, and they could be applicable to any believer, including you and me.

What is crippling you? In the next chapter, we will examine these areas in more detail and find our hope in Christ to overcome in light of God's grace. What was Jesus up to in the lives of those He sought out?

4. JACOB LIMPED

*"When the man saw that he could not overpower him, he touched the socket of Jacob's hip so that his hip was wrenched as he wrestled with the man. . . . The sun rose above him as he passed Peniel, **and he was limping because of his hip.**"* (Genesis 32:25, 31, emphasis added)

Jacob Wrestled

Jacob's wrestling match with a heavenly being resulted in a lifelong limp (Genesis 32:22-32). In addition to the limp, he received a new name in keeping with his resolve to overcome (Genesis 32:28). There are other wonderful insights to gain from Jacob's story (Genesis 32–33). When I saw the truth of his life, it changed me, and I know it will change you, too.

Jacob's name means "he grasps the heel" or "he cheats or supplants." Jacob always sought more, and he got it however he could. He had a way of getting what he wanted whether he deserved it or not. This attitude led to pain, sin, and failure. He bought his brother Esau's birthright for a bowl of soup. Then, with his mother's help, he deceived his father to obtain his father's blessing.

The Bible says that Jacob's treachery broke his brother's heart, and a family feud ensued. Jacob ran away from home because he feared for his life but found himself on the opposite end of deception by his uncle and father-in-law, Laban.

Years later, everything came to a head for Jacob. He had plans and a vision for his life. He obeyed God's direction to return home (Genesis 32:9) to his father's land in Canaan because he knew that God had promised it to him (Genesis 28:13-17).

In order to get to the promise, Jacob would have to confront his past and face his estranged brother after years of hiding in Laban's household. On his way to meet Esau, Jacob wrestled with a heavenly being. Jacob expected the worse and attempted to ease the confrontation by praying earnestly, dividing his people and his possessions into two groups, and sending peace offerings ahead of him.

Jacob was desperate and asked to be left alone. Then someone came to him. Some believe it was an angel or that it may have been Christ Himself. Either way, the Bible says that a man wrestled with Jacob until daybreak (Genesis 32:24).

> YOU MAY FEEL LIKE WRESTLING WITH GOD FOR REASONS YOU MAY NOT FULLY UNDERSTAND. GOD MAY BE BRINGING YOU TO A PLACE WHERE YOU NEED SOMETHING DESPERATELY, BUT YOU DON'T KNOW WHAT IT IS.

Jacob would not let up. When the man realized that he could not overpower Jacob, he impaired Jacob by touching the socket of his hip, which resulted in Jacob limping (Genesis 32:25, 31).

Jacob just would not let go without a blessing (Genesis 32:26). So, the man changed Jacob's name to Israel, because he had struggled with God and with men and had overcome, and then he blessed him (Genesis 32:27-28). After his struggle and the resulting limp he obtained because of his determination, Jacob received not only a blessing but a new name of destiny, a name of promise.

Struggling

Like Jacob, you may feel like wrestling with God for reasons you may not fully understand. God may be bringing you to a place where you need something desperately, but you don't know what it is. You are wrestling with something, begging God for something, but you will never get it in your own power.

The good news is that God has an answer and a blessing for you. Sometimes, however, it does not come in the way you expect it to. After a night of wrestling, the heavenly being touched Jacob's hip and put it out of joint. After praying all night, Jacob was touched by God so that he limped.

God in His great love was giving Jacob just what he needed. His limp was a physical illustration of a spiritual reality and a foretelling of the sort of limping conditions that Jesus came to heal in the New Testament for the rest of mankind. Jacob had too many limps to count, but God was bringing that into focus for him.

A limp can be mental, spiritual, or emotional. It can be caused by your own sin or by someone else's. When evil happens in you, to you, or through you, it results in pain, sin, and failure for you and for others. Our minds and spirits are then thrown into a state of limping, and we begin to lose heart.

Jacob had been limping for a long time. He had sinned against others, and he had been sinned against. But now, all of that changed. God gave Jacob the power to start walking with limps.

After Jacob's encounter with the heavenly being, Esau arrived with his band of 400 men. The Bible says, "Esau ran to meet Jacob and embraced him; he threw his arms around [Jacob's] neck and kissed him. And they wept" (Genesis 33:4). Jacob, now Israel, limped toward Esau. He couldn't fake it anymore, so he would have to trust God alone and walk with his limps. He could not help himself, and God now lavished blessings on Jacob.

> HOW ARE YOU GOING TO DEAL WITH THE "ESAUS" IN YOUR LIFE—THE PAIN, SIN, AND FAILURE ATTACHED TO THE LIMPS YOU'VE ACQUIRED? GOD WANTS YOU TO START WALKING WITH THE LIMPS THAT THESE SITUATIONS HAVE PRODUCED.

God answered Jacob unconventionally, humbling him with a limp.

It Was Necessary

Jacob's story is no different from yours or mine. His limp seemed to be a necessary progression in his life toward obtaining what God intended for him and for us. He needed to deal with his limps before he could deal with Esau.

How are you going to deal with the "Esaus" in your life—the pain, sin, and failure attached to the limps you've acquired? God wants you to start walking with the limps that these situations have produced. He gives us what we need to overcome.

- emotional limps
- sin and temptation limps
- unbelief limps
- dream limps
- accident and incident limps
- relationship limps
- illness and imperfection limps
- persecution limps

Perhaps you were abandoned or abused. Maybe you have experienced the pain of divorce or the death of a loved one. Like Jacob's hip was struck, your life has been struck in a way that has caused you to limp, and the pain of it is yet to go away. God wants to use that limp. If you deal with it as God directs, then He can bless you and others.

Perhaps a destructive sin has always plagued you and resulted in a limp of some kind. As you walk in repentance, God will enable you to walk with your limp into your destiny just as Jacob did.

Perhaps you think you aren't pretty enough or handsome enough or you feel overweight or too skinny. Remember that God made you. Maybe you have a limp of feeling imperfect. God will help you walk with this limp for His glory.

If your limping condition has worn you down, follow Jacob's example and hold on to hope in the Lord until you receive your blessing. God is more than able to help you walk with limps, as He works everything out for the good of those who love Him, those called according to His purpose (Romans 8:28).

It's time to find out more about your limps so you can get moving and be blessed. The Bible never says that Jacob's physical limp went away. Neither are we promised that our physical, emotional, or spiritual limps will go away. But Jesus promises that He'll be with us no matter what our condition is, and He will enable us to overcome.

God assured Jacob that he was going to be blessed and was leading him to Canaan to fulfill that promise, but He knew that Jacob needed to learn to walk in humility and in submission to His way. God was already at work on Jacob's behalf all along the course of his life, working everything out, good and bad, for His glory.

God knows your life, and He has plans to bless you just as He had a plan for Jacob. Isn't it amazing that despite our sinful wretchedness, God's grand desire for us does not change? Jacob's limp, or rather Israel's limp, revealed more of God's intention for his life as God faithfully upheld His covenant with Abraham and Isaac by blessing him and readying him to fulfill God's plan and purpose.

5. MEPHIBOSHETH LIMPED

"Jonathan son of Saul had a son who was lame in both feet. He was five years old when the news about Saul and Jonathan came from Jezreel. His nurse picked him up and fled, but as she hurried to leave, he fell and became disabled. His name was Mephibosheth." (2 Samuel 4:4)

Mephibosheth's Saga

At first, Mephibosheth's life seemed ideal, with no limps in sight. He was born to the prince, Jonathan, King Saul's son. That made Mephibosheth a prince, too—a five-year-old second in line to be king of Israel.

Things changed for Mephibosheth. His young life was interrupted by a grave misfortune. He incurred a physical limp at the hands of someone else.

Mephibosheth's story started long before he was born (1 Samuel 20). David and Jonathan, Mephibosheth's father, were best friends enjoying life in King Saul's palace. But Saul allowed his jealousy to overwhelm him, and he tried to kill David on several occasions.

Jonathan came to David's rescue, and, in return, Jonathan asked David to treat his descendants with kindness should anything ever happen to him. David promised Jonathan that no matter what happened to his friend, he would take care of his family. So, before Mephibosheth was born, God loved him and made provisions for him because He knew fully what his life would entail.

Your story started before you were born, too. Nothing you're facing now or have faced in the past is random. God saw all the events of your life. He factored in all your imperfections, and He has made promises to you that He will fulfill if you trust Him as you're walking with your limps. No limp, impairment, or flaw is beyond God's help. It wasn't with Mephibosheth, and it isn't with you.

Mephibosheth's grandfather, Saul, became envious when he learned that David was receiving higher praise than he was for his conquests, so he sought to kill David. Then Saul's slide into despair accelerated when he disobeyed God, who had anointed him king. Saul's sins caused a domino effect on his family: his own death and the death of his son Jonathan, which caused Mephibosheth to become fatherless.

Mephibosheth's Saga Unfolds

You may be suffering because of someone else's sin. Perhaps you are reaping the consequences of someone else's infidelity, abuse, drug addiction, anger, lusts, fears, or who-knows-what. Sometimes it's our own families that cause us to limp in some way, but Jesus came to proclaim to you that you are His child. With His help, you can overcome whatever has impaired your life.

Later, David had to battle Saul, but he refused to kill him. His honor for Saul as king of Israel would not allow him to. Ultimately, the Philistines killed Saul's sons, including Jonathan; and when it was evident that he would lose the battle, Saul killed himself.

The deaths of Saul and Jonathan struck fear in Mephibosheth's nurse, causing her to flee, carrying him in her arms. In her panic, she dropped him, which made him crippled in both feet (2 Samuel 4:4).

In an instant, both of Mephibosheth's legs were crippled, and it's highly probable that he was made lame in other ways, too. He experienced grief at the loss of his father and grandfather. His social status fell. His riches and power were gone. His life had hit an all-time low.

Eventually, David became king of Israel. It was customary in the ancient Near East for kings to kill any surviving relatives of the former king. This is most likely what induced the fear in Mephibosheth's nurse that caused her frantic escape.

Family and status, although perceived to be stable, are subject to change, and for Mephibosheth they did.

Mephibosheth's nurse seemed to be trustworthy and committed to his welfare. It is possible that her actions may have been self-serving, too. Perhaps she thought that if she protected the king's grandson, she would receive a reward; but if she didn't save him, she feared she would be put to death.

Sometimes the people we depend on may be the very ones who unintentionally or intentionally let us down. Unfortunately, we all are capable of letting others down, but we can't lose sight of the sovereignty of God. We must always forgive people, no matter the intention, and remember how God works everything out for our good.

Because of his nurse, Mephibosheth had a physical limp, but God allowed him to have that limp so that He could radically change the rest of Mephibosheth's life.

Mephibosheth's Trauma

After Mephibosheth was taken into hiding, David's army went throughout the kingdom and wiped out all of David's enemies. David came to the home of the Jebusites, who lived in the city that the king wanted to make his capital, Jerusalem. As David and his army stood outside the city walls, the Jebusites yelled, "You will not get in here; even the blind and the lame can ward you off" (2 Samuel 5:6). As compassionate as David was, the Jebusites angered him with their rebellion.

David conquered the Jebusites, and because of their suggestion that lame people would repel him, he lost his perspective and came to detest the very thought of lame people: "The lame . . . [were] hated by David's soul" (2 Samuel 5:8, NASV).

This would not have been good news for a lame child and his caregivers. They had every reason to think David's heart surely was now against him. They probably felt that Mephibosheth's days were numbered, so he went into hiding. Only God could help him now.

You may have been crippled by life's tough blows and feel that you have no one to protect you. Maybe you even created some of your limps because of your own sins or unwise decisions. Who can you count on in the midst of your fear and despair? God, of course.

> THE PEOPLE WE DEPEND ON MAY BE THE VERY ONES WHO UNINTENTIONALLY OR INTENTIONALLY LET US DOWN.

God had a plan for Mephibosheth, and He has a plan for you. We may be lame in some way, but that just means that God has us right where He wants us. We can't save ourselves or "work a deal." Mephibosheth was hiding from David, but he couldn't hide from God. God was watching over him the whole time.

Mephibosheth's life went from good to bad to good, which is a lesson to us about how to walk with limps. The following list shows eight limp areas Mephibosheth might have faced or that we might encounter during life's difficulties:
- emotional trauma
- sins and temptations
- doubt and wavering belief
- unfulfilled dreams or foiled plans
- injurious accidents and incidents
- relationship problems
- illnesses and imperfections
- persecutions

This list isn't exclusive to Mephibosheth. Perhaps you can find your limps on this list, too. I can.

After I was involved in the car accident, I struggled with the temptation to be angry with God and to blame Him for what happened to me. How could He let this happen? I'd been serving Him, and then this accident stopped everything. So, I can identify with how Mephibosheth probably felt as he was hiding from King David. Despite Mephibosheth's limp, his fear, and his uncertainty about his future, God did not forget him, and neither has He forgotten us.

Mephibosheth's Restoration

After David had cursed all the lame people in his kingdom and was now safely on the throne, God rolled out His surprising plan (2 Samuel 9). God changed David's heart. The king now remembered his promise to Jonathan to take care of his descendants, and he intended to honor it.

God keeps His promises. He is absolutely faithful and will fulfill His promises to us despite our limps and imperfections. That doesn't mean we don't have a part to play in God's plans for us. We can and should do our best in everything we do, but God is the One who blesses and empowers us. We can't accomplish anything without Him.

As you reflect on what happened to Mephibosheth, note four inspirational aspects of his story.

> GOD KEEPS HIS PROMISES. HE IS ABSOLUTELY FAITHFUL AND WILL FULFILL HIS PROMISES TO US DESPITE OUR LIMPS AND IMPERFECTIONS.

King David sought out Mephibosheth, not the other way around (2 Samuel 9:3-6): "[David] asked, 'Is there no one still alive from the house of Saul to whom I can show God's kindness?' Ziba answered the king, 'There is still a son of Jonathan; he is lame in both feet.' . . . So King David had him brought from Lo Debar, from the house of Makir son of Ammiel."

And just as King David searched for Mephibosheth, Jesus comes looking for us. We often say, "I found Jesus," but Jesus wasn't the One who was lost—we were! If you are afraid and want to run and hide from Jesus, He will find you. He seeks us out because we are lost and don't know where we are. We need a Savior to find us, heal us, and protect us.

King David called Mephibosheth out of exile (2 Samuel 9:5): "So King David had [Mephibosheth] brought from Lo Debar." Instead of sending men to kill Mephibosheth, David called him out of hiding so he could bless him.

In the same way, God calls you from where you are because He plans to bless you. John 10:10 says, "I have come that they may have life, and have it to the full." If God allows you to continue to stay in exile, hidden in fear and shame, you won't be in the right place to receive His abundant blessings.

God allows you to go through certain situations so that He can give you the life He has intended for you. Are you willing to come out of exile so you can receive what God has for you, or will you allow fear to keep you in hiding?

David welcomed Mephibosheth into his presence (2 Samuel 9:11, 13): "Mephibosheth ate at David's table like one of the king's sons. . . . And Mephibosheth lived in Jerusalem, because he always ate at the king's table." Although David had promised Jonathan that he would take care of Jonathan's descendants, David, as the newly anointed king, also could have killed Mephibosheth because he was Saul's heir.

David, however, faithful to his promise, wanted to welcome Mephibosheth into his presence. And David didn't turn him away because he was lame or because he was Saul's grandson.

Jesus loves us and calls us into His presence, even when we're messed up. He still says, "Come to me" (Matthew 11:28). When David invited Mephibosheth to his table, he was humbled by his reception. Plausibly, it may have alluded his understanding of why David wanted to treat him like a prince instead of like a servant.

Jesus doesn't wait for you to fix your limps. He welcomes you just as you are. He welcomes you as a prince or a princess and treats you like a son or a daughter, not a servant. He wants to show you favor not because of anything you've done, right or wrong, but because of who your Father is and His love for you.

> JESUS DOESN'T WAIT FOR YOU TO FIX YOUR LIMPS. HE WELCOMES YOU JUST AS YOU ARE. HE WELCOMES YOU AS A PRINCE OR A PRINCESS AND TREATS YOU LIKE A SON OR A DAUGHTER, NOT A SERVANT.

Jesus is calling forth an army of people who may be in some way limping just like Mephibosheth did but who are yet important in His kingdom. He is just waiting for you to humble yourself and let Him do His work in and through you. So stop trying to hide your limp.

Acknowledge it, and allow Jesus to help you have victory in spite of it.

King David showed Mephibosheth kindness (2 Samuel 9:7): "Don't be afraid . . . for I will surely show you kindness for the sake of your father Jonathan. I will restore to you all the land that belonged to your grandfather Saul, and you will always eat at my table."

David showed extravagant kindness to Jonathan's son. Although he was lame, Mephibosheth was given all of his grandfather's land. David also assigned Saul's servants to work the land for him. And then David gave Mephibosheth a permanent seat at the royal table, which gave him many of the same benefits and privileges the king gave his own sons.

Jesus is just as extravagant in his kindness toward us. He invites us to sit at His table so that He can lavish on us all the rights and privileges that that seat entails. Jesus wants to give you the blessings of His kingdom, and He showers you with kindness so that you can come to Him, even if you must limp into His presence.

Many times, we live beneath our privilege, not understanding that God has invited us to sit at His table. God invites all to His table (Luke 13:29) so we can be confident in our place in Him and in what He has in store for us.

For Mephibosheth's Good

David didn't treat Mephibosheth as a "lowly" cripple. He treated him like a son. That's what God wants to do for you, too.

God seeks you out, brings you out of exile, welcomes you into His presence, and showers you with His extravagant kindness. So, why would you continue to reject Him? Our great God loves us despite the pain, sin, and failure that cause us to limp. We must trust in His love for us and receive His blessings.

6. JESUS IDENTIFIES WITH OUR LIMPS

"Therefore, since we have a great high priest who has ascended into heaven, Jesus the Son of God, let us hold firmly to the faith we profess. For we do not have a high priest who is unable to empathize with our weaknesses, but we have one who has been tempted in every way, just as we are—yet he did not sin. Let us then approach God's throne of grace with confidence, so that we may receive mercy and find grace to help us in our time of need." (Hebrews 4:14-16)

The psalmist wailed, "For our soul is bowed down to the dust; our belly clings to the ground. Rise up; come to our help! Redeem us for the sake of your steadfast love!" (Psalm 44:25-26, ESV). We can identify with that cry of anguish as we deal with our own limping conditions from pain, sin, and failure, but we can be assured that Jesus hears us.

Over and over the psalmist beckoned God to hear his cry. Like the psalmist, we too cry out, entreating God to deliver us, to rescue us. As we limp, we may become overwhelmed and perhaps feel all alone.

God Sent His Son Jesus for Us

God loved us enough to send His only begotten Son, Jesus, who came to earth to ransom His people. Being fully God and fully man, Jesus was able to identify with our human frailties, or limps. As our Savior, He can save our souls and also provide us with abundant life here and now, no matter what our condition is.

Jesus humbled Himself to make life better for us. According to Philippians 2:5-9, Jesus, although Himself equal with God, His Father, humbled Himself on our behalf. He became a servant being made in human likeness like us to identify with us. He made himself nothing so that He could relate to our human condition. Then He fulfilled His Father's mission and died on a cross for us. Jesus left heaven to dwell among us in order to save us from our human condition.

> AS OUR SAVIOR, JESUS CAN SAVE OUR SOULS AND ALSO PROVIDE US WITH ABUNDANT LIFE HERE AND NOW, NO MATTER WHAT OUR CONDITION IS.

Jesus didn't arrive on earth in glory and majesty as the Israelites anticipated He would. Instead, He was born into lowly circumstances, so much so that it seemed that most everyone at that time either missed or overlooked His arrival. He took on flesh and experienced every sort of temptation imaginable; so, He experienced life as we know it and was yet without sin. He understands firsthand what we face and why we limp because of what we face.

When Jesus was conceived through the Holy Ghost, His mother, Mary, was engaged but not yet married. Then He was born with a death sentence over His head as King Herod sought to kill Him. Jesus' earthly family was never wealthy; and during His earthly ministry, He was hassled constantly by authorities. On the way to the cross, Jesus' friends rejected Him, soldiers beat Him, politicians and religious leaders mocked Him, and the crowds that once lauded His arrival cursed Him.

Jesus triumphantly experienced every limping area that we will examine in this book. He experienced *emotional trauma* as He wept as others were mourning over Lazarus's death just before He raised him from the dead (John 11:35). Jesus also faced *temptation* when He was led intentionally by the Holy Spirit to be tempted by the devil (Matthew 4:1-11). Though He was without sin, He still faced the pain of being sinned against as He faced persecution and, ultimately, His crucifixion (Matthew 26:47-75; 27:11-61).

Jesus experienced, during His earthly lifetime, *unmet dreams and expectations* for Jerusalem and its residents, God's chosen people, who failed to submit to God's plan for them (Matthew 23:37). He also witnessed *accidents and incidents* such as the one mentioned in Luke 13:4 regarding the demise of some Galileans when a tower in Siloam fell on them. He experienced other incidents such as the attempts on His life, too (Matthew 2:13; Luke 4:9-12, 28-30; John 8:57-59; 10:25-39).

Jesus experienced *relationship problems*. Some of Jesus' closest relationships were plagued with problems. Judas Iscariot, one of the twelve disciples He chose, betrayed Him (Mark 14:10). James and John, also hand-picked disciples, sought power and top rank from Him (Mark 10:35-45). Peter, one of His inner circle, denied Him not once but three times (Mark 14:66-72). Thomas doubted Him (John 20:24-29), and all of them abandoned Him upon His arrest (Mark 14:50).

Jesus came face-to-face with *illnesses and imperfections*. Jesus encountered many who were sick, and He healed them (Matthew 8:2-4, 14-15; 12:0-13; 19:2; 12:15; 21:14; Mark 2:2-12; Luke 4:33-37; 6:18; 7:12-16; 13:10-17; John 5:2-9).

Jesus also suffered great *persecution*. Jesus was persecuted by His own people, led by the Pharisees and the Sadducees (Matthew 12:14; Luke 4:29-30; 23:11; John 5:16; 7:1; 8:37; 10:39).

Overcoming Through Jesus Christ

Jesus knows exactly why we limp, but He did more than come to earth to end our pain. He gave His life and became our once-for-all-sacrifice so that our sins can be forgiven and so that we can have eternal life.

On the cross, Jesus bore the sin of humanity—our ultimate limping condition. He was mocked and rejected by those He came to save; yet He endured the cross. Through Him and Him alone we can learn to walk with our limps and overcome the reality of them for His glory.

If you've sinned so much that you feel crippled and lame beyond help, this is good news for you. Jesus specializes in "sin limps," and He intercedes on our behalf before the Father.

Jesus, scarred by nail prints in His hands and feet, knows that you have scars, too. Your limping conditions have caused wounds, and although scar tissue heals over those wounds, the reality of those wounds and scars may remain evident.

I will carry to my grave many of the scars from the injuries I sustained during the car accident. Every time I touch those scars, though, they remind me of how God saved me and of my place before God.

> SCARS AREN'T ALWAYS BAD. THEY CAN BE GOD'S REMINDER TO YOU OF HOW MUCH HE LOVES YOU AND WHAT HE HAS BROUGHT YOU THROUGH.

Scars aren't always bad. They can be God's reminder to you of how much He loves you and what He has brought you through. The memory of what God has done for you can give you fresh faith to face another day of walking with your limps. Paradoxically, wholeness begins with Jesus enabling you to walk with your limps and overcome them for God's glory.

"The All Ready" and "the Not Yet"

While it is comforting to know that Christ identifies with our limps and we are confident that He will help us overcome, there exists the paradox of "the already" and "the not yet." The difficulty of dealing with "the not yet"—which means I know that I'm healed by the power of God, but my healing has not yet manifested—is a great challenge. Because of faith, we know that this too shall pass and that weeping may endure for the night, but joy comes in the morning.

> ONE OF THE MOST DIFFICULT MOMENTS WHEN DEALING WITH LIMPS IS WHEN YOU FEEL ALL ALONE, EVEN IN A CROWDED ROOM.

One problem with walking with a physical limp is that you are unable to move fast and you're unable to step over normal obstacles. For example, if a sudden downpour occurs while you're walking from a building to your car, you will get soaking wet because of your inability to make a run for it.

Also if you come to a steep set of stairs that is less than four feet from the entrance of a building, you might have to take the ramp, which requires you to travel sixteen feet before making it to the door. One must have patience and perseverance in order to walk with a limp, because walking with a limp requires more time and energy to reach your destination.

The problem with living with the different limps that we refer to in this book is that the rain and the obstacles are not physical but are abstract. For example, a person who is attempting to overcome sexual limps because of being raped hears a story on the news about a person being convicted of rape in another state. Immediately, fear resurfaces because that person's attacker was never charged or convicted.

Often times, persons dealing with the limps referred to in this book do not recognize the impact their pain is causing on family members or friends. The good news is that we have a high priest that is fully aware of our pain and gives us the confidence that we can do all things through Him.

Alone in a Crowded Room

One of the most difficult moments when dealing with limps is when you feel all alone, even in a crowded room. How is it that you feel all alone in a crowded room?

You feel all alone when the conversations that are taking place in the room are so far away from your way of thinking. You feel all alone when it appears that everyone in the room is prospering while you are attempting to survive. You feel all alone when others in the room are giving testimonies about God's blessings on their lives while you are barely getting by. When you are feeling alone in a crowded room, it is important to remember that you are never alone.

Thank Me Now

The Lord taught me a great lesson while I was recovering from my physical injuries that has enabled me to overcome the types of limps referred to in this book. On this particular night, Tracy had gone through the routine of feeding me, bathing me, helping me into my pajamas, taking care of the boys, and giving me my medication. Her willingness to take care of me humbled and shamed me in ways that I cannot describe in this book.

Regardless of how I tried to move, I could not find a comfortable position because my pain was excruciating. All I could do was roll out of the bed and hold myself up on the dresser because I was unable to stand without any assistance. I began to cry out to God like the writer described in many of the Psalms. The physical pain was so great I was literally wishing for death, which is a prime example of how my physical limp revealed that I had mental and emotional limps as well.

That night, as I stood there looking in the mirror with tears streaming down my face, I felt the Lord say, "Thank Me now, and until you thank Me, you will never have any relief."

The problem was I didn't know what I could possibly be thanking God for at that time. He told me to thank Him for my pain and suffering because it was molding me more into His image. He told me to thank Him for my healing as if it was already done. It's amazing that as I began to praise Him and worship Him, I began to realize that God was going to restore every part of my life.

It has been a long, painful process with many setbacks along the way. However, one lesson I learned that carries me today is that we must praise God despite our circumstances. The peace that surpasses all understanding just might be one praise away.

7. SOCIAL LIMPS

"Come, see a man who told me everything I ever did. Could this be the Messiah?" (John 4:29).

Tommie could hear his sister crying in the next room as his father beat his mother for cheating on him. The youngest of six children, Tommie longed for attention in this harsh environment, and he found that he could get it by being a troublemaker.

He became his first-grade teacher's worst nightmare. By second grade, Tommie had already been suspended twelve times. His teacher told his parents that he made her consider quitting teaching, and he was kicked out of school again and again.

By fifth grade, Tommie had attended six schools. When older street kids brought him into their gang, they offered him a perverse sense of acceptance. The gang stole bicycles and sold the parts. Then Tommie was arrested. During this time, his parents divorced, and his mother bounced around to several hospitals due to mental illness.

"All I ever wanted was attention," he said.

What About You?

Amid terrible social realities, Tommie was headed down a one-way street to failure.

Have you ever felt like that?

Like Tommie, maybe your parents divorced, setting you on a wrong path. Perhaps you felt unattractive, pulling away from peers and into a downward spiral of loneliness. Maybe you have been subjected to prejudices from society based on your background, race, or socio-economic status that caused you to feel inferior.

> SATAN'S DESTRUCTIVE PLANS KEEP YOU FROM LIMPING TOWARD GOD. YOU HAVE A CHOICE: LIMP FOR SATAN, OR LIMP FOR GOD.

Social Limps Hit Everyone

For Tommie, the limps of a dysfunctional family, a troubled school record, and gangster friends kept getting worse. Like Tommie, his siblings also had their own issues, one dropping out of school and another becoming a thief. Tommie had basketball skills, but he spent most of his time with his gang. He put gold crowns on his teeth and got 52 tattoos, copying his street brothers and saying to the rest of the world, "Deal with it!"

As an underage driver, Tommie was jailed for joy-riding. Schools kept passing him from one grade to the other even though he failed all of his classes. He sold drugs and carried a gun.

He got angry—really angry.

Inside, Tommie still felt a tug to make something positive of his life, and basketball was his ticket. When he played, he even made his father proud. He played on a traveling team but remained part of a negative social world. Finally, he was jailed in a youth detention center for 20 days for selling drugs.

When Tommie was moved to another school, a teacher there shared the gospel with him. Finally, he felt God doing something in his life. He started making passing grades in school and spent more time at basketball practice. Now when he played, he made friends and gained a renewed perspective on life.

But despite all of the good things happening in his life, Tommie and a friend broke into a store. The police shot his friend five times, and he died hours later. Tommie got away. *That could have been me*, Tommie thought. He had been limping back and forth between hope and hopelessness, and this time, it caught up with him.

Have you tried to break out of your social problems only to end up limping worse? Satan's destructive plans keep you from limping toward God. You have a choice: Limp for Satan, or limp for God. You can overcome your limps with God's help, allowing Him to use them for His glory.

Has Satan convinced you that you can't get out of the destructive social patterns? But you've heard God calling you, inviting you to become a member of Jesus' limping warriors, His army of believers. One day, you feel utter hopelessness; the next day, you experience an unusual sense of hope in your spirit.

Your destructive social past or present does not have to define you. You can break free.

The Problem

A social limp is the result of destructive people, situations, and environments. Your limp pulls you down and tempts you to give up and wallow in self-pity.

Some people's limps are obvious: For example, they were born on the "wrong side of town," perhaps living in gross poverty. Other people's limps might not be as apparent. Perhaps they find themselves in a hostile work environment or among friends who have betrayed them.

Your limp might come from anything: abusive or addicted parents, a single-parent household, chaotic childhood. No matter the origin of your limp, learn to use it for Jesus. Instead of making excuses for your actions, lean on Jesus, and limp in His power and strength.

Satan wants your limp to trip you up and send you crashing to the ground, but Jesus wants to lift you up and use your limps for His glory. Like Jesus, Jacob, Paul, and Mephibosheth, you can enter Jesus' army of limping soldiers. You will find acceptance there. Refuse to continue to rationalize or excuse your condition. Trust God to use your limps for a higher purpose, and God will turn your limps into blessings for you and for others.

Facing Jesus

Jesus decided to travel through Samaria on His way to Galilee. He was tired and thirsty, so He stopped at a place that was revered by Jews and Samaritans: Jacob's well. There, he saw a Samaritan woman and asked her to draw water for him to drink.

The Samaritan woman was incredulous. As indicated by her response, she was skeptical about His request.

In biblical times, Jews and Samaritans avoided socializing with each other because Jews looked down on Samaritans as a mixed breed of people. There was so much animosity between the two groups that the Jews took the long road around Samaria so they wouldn't have to interact with Samaritans at all. In addition, in ancient Near Eastern culture, neither ethnic group thought it appropriate to talk to women in public because women were thought of as second-class citizens.

> TRUST GOD TO USE YOUR LIMPS FOR A HIGHER PURPOSE, AND GOD WILL TURN YOUR LIMPS INTO BLESSINGS FOR YOU AND FOR OTHERS.

The woman said, "You are a Jew and I am a Samaritan woman. How can you ask me for a drink?"

Jesus answered her, "If you knew the gift of God and who it is that asks you for a drink, you would have asked him and he would have given you living water" (John 4:9-10).

The Samaritan woman had two obvious social limps imposed on her by the culture in which she lived when Jesus approached her: her ethnicity and her gender. But neither of these limps stopped Jesus from talking to her about the living water He was offering.

> YOU CAN'T HIDE YOUR SOCIAL SINS FROM JESUS AND THEN EXPLAIN THEM AWAY ONCE HE REVEALS THEM. JESUS CAN SEE THROUGH YOUR LIMPS, AND HE WANTS TO HELP YOU OVERCOME THEM.

Jesus could have taken the long road around, but He intentionally went through Samaria because He wanted an encounter with this limping woman. Nothing could keep Him away from her—not her social status, her ethnicity, or her gender.

Jesus will do the same for you. He doesn't go out of His way to avoid you. Instead, He'll go anywhere to encounter you and help you limp for Him. He'll enter a drug den, an abusive marriage, a hospital room, and anywhere else He has to go just to find you.

As Jesus looked into the Samaritan woman's eyes, He saw past her visible limps. He also saw that she was locked in destructive social circumstances, and He spoke directly to them. How could Jesus reach out to such a wretched person? Because Jesus "came to seek and to save the lost" (Luke 19:10). He came to bring healing to all who needed it.

In response, the woman did the same thing we often do. She immediately began making excuses. She even cloaked her excuses in biblical language, but she was no match for Jesus. He moved beyond her social limps and excuses and dug deeper to her invisible limp.

"Go, call your husband and come back," Jesus said.

"I have no husband," she replied.

"You are right when you say you have no husband," Jesus said. "The fact is, you have had five husbands, and the man you now have is not your husband. What you have just said is quite true" (John 4:16-18).

Like this woman, you can't hide your social sins from Jesus and then explain them away once He reveals them. Jesus can see through your limps, and He wants to help you overcome them.

Jesus might have seemed tough on the woman at the well, but she had to face the hard facts. Whether she liked it or not, her excuses and complaining would not be tolerated. She had to see things the way they were: the biblical way. She had to repent.

"Sir," the woman said, "I can see that you are a prophet. Our ancestors worshiped on this mountain, but you Jews claim that the place where we must worship is in Jerusalem."

"Woman," Jesus replied, "believe me, a time is coming when you will worship the Father neither on this mountain nor in Jerusalem. You Samaritans worship what you do not know; we worship what we do know, for salvation is from the Jews" (John 4:19-22).

Jesus didn't accept the woman's excuses. Instead, he told her what she and every Samaritan hated to hear but had to admit: "Salvation is from the Jews." Jesus' words might seem harsh to us, but the truth of Scripture can't be altered. You can't be saved any way but God's way. The only way to be set free was and is through Christ.

The Samaritan woman finally stopped excusing her limps. At that point, she was about to face the biggest decision of her life. Jesus was going to call her to turn over her limps, or rather, her life, to him and enter God's divine redemption and restoration program. Once she exhausted her excuses and her denial of God's only way for salvation, she was ready to hear the good news:

> Yet a time is coming and has now come when the true worshipers will worship the Father in the Spirit and in truth, for they are the kind of worshipers the Father seeks. God is spirit, and his worshipers must worship in the Spirit and in truth. The woman said, "I know that Messiah" (called Christ) "is coming. When he comes, he will explain everything to us." Then Jesus declared, "I, the one speaking to you—I am he." (John 4:23-26)

It Is Safe to Limp Toward God

The woman at the well faced the ultimate decision. Would she limp toward him or away from him? She could bow to Jesus or limp back the way she came.

We all face such decisions. When Jesus comes to us with the truth, sometimes it seems we'd rather remain in our ungodly lifestyles, but that's what keeps us stuck where we are—unsatisfied and limping miserably.

It is time for you to stop limping in your social reality and start glorifying God in His heavenly reality. Become part of Jesus' limping army so you can see God's purpose for your life. He wants to give every believer new strength and new hope.

It is safe to limp toward God, drawing near to Him, and to begin living for God. The Scriptures promise you that God will be with you in your valley:

> THE TRUTH OF SCRIPTURE CAN'T BE ALTERED. YOU CAN'T BE SAVED ANY WAY BUT GOD'S WAY. THE ONLY WAY TO BE SET FREE IS THROUGH CHRIST.

> The LORD is my shepherd, I lack nothing. He makes me lie down in green pastures, he leads me beside quiet waters, he refreshes my soul. He guides me

along the right paths for his name's sake. Even though I walk through the darkest valley, I will fear no evil, for you are with me; your rod and your staff, they comfort me. (Psalm 23:1-4)

What is the valley like? This passage clearly states that it is dark and full of evil. But God is there in the valley to help, to guide, and to heal.

In Psalm 23, God promises us three things:

God is our protector. His rod and staff comfort us (verse 4). In biblical times, a shepherd used a rod and a staff to protect his flock. If a lion or a wolf entered the flock, the shepherd battled them away with the rod and staff. That is how Jesus treats our enemies. What a comfort this can be for us.

God is our provider. He brings us into green pastures and quiet waters, and He refreshes our souls (verse 2). God will keep us safe, even in the midst of evil. Limps may beset us, but God is beside us, comforting and healing and giving us hope.

> GOD WILL KEEP US SAFE, EVEN IN THE MIDST OF EVIL. LIMPS MAY BESET US, BUT GOD IS BESIDE US, COMFORTING AND HEALING AND GIVING US HOPE.

God is our preserver. Shepherds also used the rod and the staff to keep the sheep from wandering. If a sheep began to stray from the safety of the flock, the shepherd used the crook on the staff to gently hook the sheep's neck and draw it back into the fold. Jesus saves us from falling any further. He is with us as we limp through the valley, and He will help us to limp safely and surely alongside Him.

How do you handle a social limp? The world offers government assistance, protests, excuses, and a plethora of other things that might give you temporary help. But this book offers you a more personal, Bible-based line of action for becoming a social limper in Jesus' army, a member of His body of believers. The best way to learn how to limp for Jesus through your social trials is to activate the three R's: *Report* your limp, *rejoice* in your social limp, and *reason* regarding your social limp.

Report Your Limp

Don't try to explain, excuse, or hide your limp. Instead, report it to God in prayer: "Lord, I have a social limp, and it is _____." Report it to your pastor or your spouse. By report, I don't mean to file a report as you would at work. Just state it clearly: "My limp is _____ because _____, and this is my pain."

Jesus suffered, and we must suffer, too: "For Christ also suffered once for sins, the righteous for the unrighteous, to bring you to God. He was put to death in the body but made alive in the Spirit" (1 Peter 3:18). Jesus suffered, and He identifies with our limps. He captured the agony of His suffering when He prayed so earnestly to God His Father, asking Him for the removal of "this cup"—the cross.

Second Timothy 2:12 says, "If we endure, we will also reign with him. If we disown him, he will also disown us." Jesus isn't asking you to do anything that He hasn't already done. He suffered with our limps in the garden, and He is calling us to do the same with His help and for His glory.

So, report your limp. Once you do, you will no longer need to go one-on-one with it alone. You now have the prayer and the counsel of others on your side.

Paul reported his limp when he wrote to other churches asking for their prayers about the thorn in his flesh. He didn't hide it; he reported it.

Following her encounter with Jesus, the woman at the well reported her limp to herself and to others. In Psalm 23:4, God promises to protect, provide, and preserve His people. You need to quit trying on your own to do these things and start accepting Jesus' offer to do them through you.

The woman at the well is an example of someone who lived out reporting her limp. John 4:28-29, 39-42 says,

> Leaving her water jar, the woman went back to the town and said to the people, "Come, see a man who told me everything I ever did. Could

this be the Messiah? . . . Many of the Samaritans from that town believed in him because of the woman's testimony, "He told me everything I ever did." So when the Samaritans came to him, they urged him to stay with them, and he stayed two days. And because of his words many more became believers. They said to the woman, "We no longer believe just because of what you said; now we have heard for ourselves, and we know that this man really is the Savior of the world."

> JESUS ISN'T ASKING YOU TO DO ANYTHING THAT HE HASN'T ALREADY DONE. HE SUFFERED WITH OUR LIMPS IN THE GARDEN, AND HE IS CALLING US TO DO THE SAME WITH HIS HELP AND FOR HIS GLORY.

She reported the reality that she was a limper. She stopped making excuses or trying to hide her limp. She went straight into her town and said, "Come, see a man who told me everything I ever did. Could this be the Messiah?"

The rest of the passage indicates that she knew he was the Messiah. She had yielded to him. The Bible says that "many more [in the town] became believers." She was the first in town to admit her reality and believe in Jesus.

Don't make excuses or hide your limp like the woman at the well did initially. Admit the social limps in your life, and tell God that you can't handle them alone. With Jesus' power, you can handle them.

Rejoice in Your Limp

In the past, you've probably responded to limps by wallowing, complaining, and whining in self-pity. That is just where Satan wanted you because you were limping for him in sin and its guilt and consequences. But once you admit the reality of your limp, things change. Now you can, and should, rejoice.

Romans 5:3 says, "We also glory in our sufferings, because we know that suffering produces perseverance." Don't groan in the middle of your situation. Rejoice that God is with you. Your limps are making you like Jesus because they are producing perseverance.

The woman at the well rejoiced in her limp. The Bible says that after she admitted her reality, "many of the Samaritans from that town believed in him because of the woman's testimony, . . . They said

> DON'T MAKE EXCUSES OR HIDE YOUR LIMP. ADMIT THE SOCIAL LIMPS IN YOUR LIFE, AND TELL GOD THAT YOU CAN'T HANDLE THEM ALONE. WITH JESUS' POWER, YOU CAN HANDLE THEM.

to the woman, 'We no longer believe just because of what you said; now we have heard for ourselves.' "

Can't you just see the joy in her eyes? Can you sense how she must have bubbled up with infectious happiness? She rejoiced.

Sometimes we need to praise God out loud and tell others what we are understanding spiritually in our heart. When we do, it solidifies that truth and reality, and it supernaturally gives that truth power to work in us. She gave her testimony to others, and you can bet that she rejoiced as she spoke. She announced her new reality. The people in her town went from seeing a sad, ungodly woman to seeing a joyful, enthusiastic one. The supernatural truth was at work in her.

Reason Regarding Your Limp

Psalm 30:5 says, "Weeping may stay for the night, but rejoicing comes in the morning." Memorize this verse and other verses that encourage you, and repeat them to yourself when you feel like giving up. When you do, you are speaking God's truth to the problem and thwarting the enemy.

Isaiah 1:18 says, "Come now, let us reason together" (NKJV). God is inviting you to reason with Him in thoughtful conversation. He wants to use your brain and apply your spiritual understanding.

Use your reasoning abilities to counter your unpredictable emotions. Tell yourself that your limp may last for weeks, months, years, or the rest of your life, but joy will come. The night of your limp will yield to the morning of now and the rest of your eternal life because your perspective about your condition will change.

Isaiah 1:18 ends with, "Though your sins are like scarlet, they shall be as white as snow. Though they are red like crimson, they shall be as wool." When we reason with God, He tells us not only what we need to know about our heart but also informs our head that our limping is not in vain. He reminds us that He has cleansed us.

God can use your limp for good, which will bring you joy in this life. You will also experience joy in the life hereafter. Matthew 25:21 says that when you and I see Jesus, He will say, "Well done, good and faithful servant! You have been faithful with a few things; I will put you in charge of many things. Come and share your master's happiness!"

That is real, everlasting joy! The long-term outcome of limping for Jesus is far better than the short-lived outcome of limping for Satan.

Reason with confidence. Psalm 23:4 says that when you are in the valley, limping for Jesus, don't fear evil. Be confident. Don't fear the hardships and pains that society can put on you. Jesus is with you.

In Matthew 28:20, Christ promises us, "Surely I am with you always, to the very end of the age."

Jesus is on your side.

The woman at the well reasoned regarding her limp. Jesus offered her living water. She thought it over, and after hearing Jesus explain what this water was, she took it. Jesus offered her a new way of looking at herself.

This woman perhaps said to herself: "This all adds up. I'm all in." That was the extent of her reasoning processes.

Jesus took up for her when his disciples put her down. The Bible says, "Just then his disciples returned and were surprised to find him talking with a woman" (John 4:27).

They never told him this, but their faces and reactions said it all. But Jesus was in the woman's camp. She was on mission. He knew that his disciples often jumped to quick conclusions, and they needed to break free from their preconceived stereotypes and prejudices.

The woman had reasoned better than Jesus' disciples had.

> "THOUGH YOUR SINS ARE LIKE SCARLET, THEY SHALL BE AS WHITE AS SNOW. THOUGH THEY ARE RED LIKE CRIMSON, THEY SHALL BE AS WOOL."
> (ISAIAH 1:18)

A Whole New Ballgame

Tommie excelled as he continued to play basketball, but one night, he fell back in with the wrong crowd. His friends invited him to skip school, and as he was hanging out with them, he heard gunshots. One of his friends got hit, and then Tommie felt pain in his foot. He had been shot, too.

Tommie almost lost his foot, and the doctor told him he might never play basketball again. Tommie was heartbroken. He lay in bed for three weeks, crying in self-pity.

His father told him to stop feeling sorry for himself. "If God has plans, nothing can get in the way of that," he told his son.

"I felt every word," Tommie recalls.

So, Tommie got out of bed and started hobbling on crutches. He surrounded himself with the right people. He worked out at five in the morning, doing his best to rehabilitate his foot. He was now limping for Jesus.

When basketball season came, his coach and his friends thought he was crazy to try to play, but Tommie ignored them. To show them he was serious about making a comeback, he got a tattoo on his arm that said "Only the strong survive" and one on his neck that said "God is good."

In his first game, Tommie was in severe pain, but he scored 30 points and thanked God for allowing him to play. He started studying, earning A's and B's and only one D, and colleges started recruiting him.

Then Tommie met a motivational speaker named Tommie Ford, who told him, "Never use your background as an excuse not to succeed. You can be whatever you want to if you put forth the effort."

Tommie now recalls, "I just allowed God to steer."

He spoke to local youth groups. Though his grades were still low, a junior college accepted him on scholarship. He continued to apply himself, and Missouri State University gave him a scholarship.

Everything seemed to be looking up for Tommie when he was accused of cheating on a college exam. The teacher, who saw his tattoos and gold teeth, assumed he could not have made a 94. Tommie could have given up and gone back to his old ways, but he persevered. The teacher forced him to retake a different version of the test, and he aced that one, too. In tears, the teacher asked Tommie to forgive her for judging him negatively.

Tommie became a star. Kids wanted his autograph. His picture was everywhere, and he was on TV. Then he hurt his back lifting weights. He could have limped back into Satan's army, but he kept limping for Jesus. He came back and starred again on the MSU basketball team.

Then another shock came. His beloved coach announced he was leaving MSU. The new coach brought in his own players, and Tommie had to switch back to a junior college. There, he fell back into his old ways; but he repented and kept limping for Jesus.

In time, Tommie wanted to return to his roots in Mississippi. He tried out for the team at Tougaloo College, a prestigious black school that was pivotal in the Civil Rights movement. He made the team on full scholarship. Tommie began to grow in the Lord again. He starred at Tougaloo, and he committed himself to helping struggling students at a local school.

The faculty and administration put Tommie on key student boards. Then he decided to run for Mr. Tougaloo. Most everyone told him he was crazy, but he won!

When Tommie spoke to the college's new freshman class, some of them asked how he could be Mr. Tougaloo with gold teeth and tattoos. By this time, Tommie was again attending my church, New Jerusalem Church in Jackson, and I was mentoring him. He came to me for advice about whether he should remove his gold teeth.

"That's a good idea," I said. We (the church along with myself) were happy to pay for the procedure.

Today, Tommie Mabry teaches in the Jackson Public School System, where students look up to him as a role model. He is a popular speaker, giving his testimony and seeing God save many children. If you want to learn more about Tommie's story, read his book, *A Dark Journey to a Light Future* (tommiemabry.wix.com). This book is changing lives.

Despite his success, Tommie still bears the scars of the wounds inflicted from his past. He has limps from bad decisions he made, but he is now limping for Jesus, and Jesus is using him. His smile is infectious, and he declares his testimony by the power of God's Spirit.

If God can change Tommie, he can change you. He will turn your limp from a defect to an asset for His kingdom. Let God take the painful limps of your past and turn them into promising opportunities for your present and your future.

8. EMOTIONAL LIMPS

"They will have no fear of bad news; their hearts are steadfast, trusting in the LORD." (Psalm 112:7)

After years of abuse, Dennis's father and mother had been separated for months. But that fateful day, he emerged from the bathroom with a gun in his hand.

"If I can't have you, then ain't no one else gonna have you!" he said and then shot Dennis's mother six times. She lay dead in a pool of blood.

At the time, Dennis was a few blocks away at his friend's house. Although he was the youngest of five children, at 15 years old, he had proven to be the toughest and bravest of his siblings when it came to standing up for his mother. When Dennis was 13, his father had stabbed his mother six times, and he constantly beat Dennis, who had learned to fight back.

Now his mother was dead, and Dennis seethed with hatred. "I had one thing on my mind when I heard that he had killed her. I wanted to find him and kill him."

But before Dennis could track him down, his father gave himself up to the police. Dennis was left dreaming of and wishing for revenge. He was filled with hatred and anger, which he carried with him for decades.

It's normal to experience a range of emotions, good and bad. However, left unchecked, these emotions can attach themselves to us like leeches and suck the life from us. They can appear unannounced like a cancer, spreading death to our souls. Emotions can also cause psychological limps that Satan will use to keep us from living a fulfilled Christian life.

> FEELING NEGATIVE EMOTIONS IS NORMAL. WE CAN'T ESCAPE THEM BECAUSE WE LIVE IN A FALLEN AND BROKEN WORLD, AND MANY TIMES LIFE HITS US WITH CIRCUMSTANCES BEYOND OUR CONTROL.

The Problem

When God created us in His image, He designed us to embody many of His characteristics and display similar emotions. So, when Adam and Eve inhabited the garden, they must have experienced many good emotions such as awe, confidence, happiness, curiosity, love, gratitude, pleasure, hope, joy, trust, and love.

After Adam and Eve sinned and were banished from the garden, these healthy, desirable emotions may have given way to more negative feelings. The couple then most likely faced a different range of emotions that reflected their fall, including anger, grief, worry, hatred, apathy, despair, sadness, fear, regret, disappointment, hurt, shame, loneliness, lust, and remorse. These emotions are common to the human race today and cause us to limp in ways that take us off course from where God intends us to go.

Our limps are a result of carrying too much emotional baggage from the way others have treated us and from the way we have treated others. Our limps come from our failures, our weaknesses, our sicknesses, and our disappointments. These limps can take us down the road to destruction, or they can be used by Jesus to mold us into His humble servants.

Emotions in and of themselves are neutral. Our emotions typically can be categorized in one of three ways: sad, mad, or glad. For example, when mad, we may display envy, jealousy, and hatred. When sad, we may experience despair, hopelessness, and self-pity. And when glad, we may project joy, peace, and love. What's inside you or Who's inside you will determine what role emotions will play in your life.

Feeling negative emotions is normal. We can't escape them because we live in a fallen and broken world, and many times life hits us with circumstances beyond our control. That does not mean, however, that we should be controlled by our emotions. When we surrender to negativity, our emotions cripple us and cause us to limp. So we must address our negative emotions if we are going to grow as emotionally healthy human beings.

Our emotions should be ruled by the Spirit rather than by our flesh. When emotions are ruled by the flesh, they can be sinful or negative; but when they are ruled by God's Spirit, they can be a blessing.

Jesus was tempted to give into the same negative emotions we face. The Bible says he "shared in their humanity" (Hebrews 2:14) and that "he himself suffered when he was tempted" (Hebrews 2:18). Jesus was "sorrowful and troubled" (Matthew 26:37), and He wept (John 11:35). The good news is that "He is able to help those who are being tempted" (Hebrews 2:18). That includes the temptation to be ruled by negative emotions.

When you feel tempted to surrender to negative emotions, Jesus is there to help you overcome that emotional vise grip and enter a better state of mind. This does not mean you will never fall back into an emotional rut. You may very well limp again unless God chooses to deliver you—and most often He will if you ask Him to.

Then there are times when we may experience purposeful or intentional pain in our relationship with Jesus. Sometimes, the only way He can draw us closer is by using pain to get our attention, which causes us to see where we've veered from the path He has designated for us. Although we limp, we can be delivered from pain and suffering with Christ's help.

Relationships Create Emotional Limps

Most of our emotions are usually connected to our relationships. Relationships produce good and bad emotions between spouses, siblings, friends, or co-workers; but in solid relationships, the good emotions prevail. Weak relationships usually produce bad emotions unless the people involved address the source of the negativity and work to overcome it.

Smokey Robinson's song "I Second That Emotion" reminds us that we should be careful what emotions we "second." That is, we should be careful about approving of the wrong emotions. Validation of the wrong emotions allows them to take root destructively in our hearts and minds.

> WE SHOULD BE CAREFUL ABOUT APPROVING OF THE WRONG EMOTIONS. VALIDATION OF THE WRONG EMOTIONS ALLOWS THEM TO TAKE ROOT DESTRUCTIVELY IN OUR HEARTS AND MINDS.

Jesus was saddened after learning that His friend Lazarus had died and that Lazarus's sisters were grieving (John 11). Two days after receiving news of Lazarus's death, Jesus finally arrived at Mary and Martha's house and met them in their grief. He entered their emotional pain, but he didn't linger there. He went straight to the source of their grief: Lazarus's tomb.

Like Mary, we tend to want to linger in our sadness or in any intense emotion such as anger. Instead, we should allow Christ to work in us to deal head-on with our emotions.

Although moved Himself by Lazarus's death and the resulting grief of others, Jesus went to the source of the pain, going to the tomb and calling Lazarus forth. Despite being dead for four days, being dressed and bound for burial, Lazarus came out of the tomb. Jesus dealt with the source of grief and performed a miraculous solution all for the glory of God.

Emotionally Equipped

Our emotions come and go, and they don't always follow a logical path. We can be happy, then sad, then glad, then angry, and then back to happy—all in the same day. We can follow Christ's example and exercise self-control in our emotions when we know God's truth and adhere to it.

> IN ORDER TO OVERCOME OUR EMOTIONS, WE MUST TURN OUR EYES AWAY FROM OUR CIRCUMSTANCES AND FOCUS ON JESUS CHRIST. HE HAS GIVEN US EVERYTHING WE NEED TO BE VICTORIOUS.

In this life, we will experience tragedies, failures, and broken relationships, but if we are in the Word and limping with Jesus, He will guide our emotions to a state of joy and peace. With Christ's help, we can control our emotions instead of letting them control us, and we can produce more godly characteristics:

"But the fruit of the Spirit is love, joy, peace, forbearance, kindness, goodness, faithfulness, gentleness and self-control. Against such things there is no law" (Galatians 5:22-23).

Prayer has always been a saint's best strategy when flooded with emotions. When David was hunted by Saul and when he felt the pain of his own sin, he prayed. He cried out to God, and God helped him. Despite the miracles God performed through Elijah, the prophet became depressed. But he prayed, and God met him in his pain and delivered him.

Like many of the greatest people in the Bible, you too will have tomb experiences; but you can also have peace and joy when hard times come. The Bible says to "consider it pure . . . whenever you face trials of many kinds" (James 1:2). Psalm 112:7 says, "They will have no fear of bad news; their hearts are steadfast, trusting in the LORD."

In order to overcome our emotions, we must turn our eyes away from our circumstances and focus on Jesus Christ. He has given us everything we need to be victorious. We need only push past ourselves, denying ourselves and following His ways.

Jesus' disciples were elated when Jesus performed amazing miracles, but they were indignant and perplexed when Jesus talked to tax collectors or Samaritans. They were happy to be in Jesus' presence, but they were sad and afraid when He was laid in the tomb.

Dealing With Emotional Limps

Christ stands ready to lift you up off the mat of emotional limps and put you on the road to limping for Him, but there's a part you must play.

Admit when you are struggling with your emotions. Admittedly, this can be difficult because you will come face to face with acknowledging that there may be something wrong with you. Often, others help us by pointing out our emotional struggle, especially when we get stuck "in our feelings."

When we don't own up to our emotions and the intent of our hearts to ourselves and others, we set ourselves up to be influenced by the enemy and thereby led into sin. The Bible has a godly answer for every unchecked emotion. If we keep God and all that He has made possible for us through Christ and live Holy Spirit-filled lives, no negative emotion will be able to continue to overtake us.

If you feel that you are being controlled by certain negative emotions or feelings and that your life and those around you are being adversely affected by them, then yield to Christ and take time to listen to the Holy Spirit. Jesus says, "Come to me, all you who are weary and burdened, and I will give you rest" (Matthew 11:28).

Are your emotions wearing you out? Try praying this prayer: "Lord Jesus, I am weary and burdened by my emotions. I come to you. Give me your rest. In Jesus' name. Amen."

That's what Dennis did, and it changed his emotional life.

Emotional Healing

Dennis was outraged when his father killed his mother.

"It was rough," he recalls. For years after her death, all he could think was, *My dad is going to get out one day, and I'm going to kill him.*

By the time Dennis was in his thirties, anger, bitterness, and revenge controlled his heart. And he asked himself, *Who is God? And if there is a God, why would He let my daddy kill my mama?*

One day, Dennis visited my church.

"I liked the way Pastor Pickett spoke," Dennis said. After attending several services, he started going to a men's Bible study. Eventually, Dennis told me his story. I told him that unless he could see that God had a purpose in it all, he would remain locked in a prison of negative emotions. He needed to see God's love for him. I told him that if he had been at the house when his mother was killed, his father might have killed him, too.

> THE BIBLE HAS A GODLY ANSWER FOR EVERY UNCHECKED EMOTION. YIELD TO CHRIST AND TAKE TIME TO LISTEN TO THE HOLY SPIRIT.

I encouraged Dennis to pray so that he could release his anger and see God's plan for his life. Then he realized that his negative emotions ought to be replaced with forgiveness and with gratitude that God had saved him.

"That is when I started waking up," he said.

When his father was in the hospital with a feeding tube in his throat, Dennis visited him. He looked at his dying father and said, "I forgive you." Unable to speak, his father just squeezed his hand. Dennis's emotional bondage was broken!

"I feel a whole lot better. Today, the situation doesn't bother me anymore," Dennis says.

Today, Dennis is over 50 years old, married with six children, and still attends my church. He loves his children and his wife, and they love him. The emotional curse has been broken in his family.

You don't have to let emotional limps, emotional trauma, lead you into destruction. If you remain in Christ and He remains in you, if you yield your whole being to Him and trust Him fully, if you follow Christ's example in all He faced on earth and accept the testimonies of other believers who have been delivered like Dennis has been, then you too can be delivered from any emotional grip.

9. SEXUAL LIMPS

"No temptation has overtaken you except what is common to mankind. And God is faithful; he will not let you be tempted beyond what you can bear. But when you are tempted, he will also provide a way out so that you can endure it." (1 Corinthians 10:13)

Until I started writing this book, I had never told anyone about the sexual molestation I endured growing up. Both of my parents died without knowing. As close as I am to my brother, I'd never told him.

I never told anybody.

As a result, I built up shame and all its consequences.

When I was six, babysitters molested me. I felt so filthy that I got into a scalding hot tub of water because I wanted to wash that sick feeling off me. It felt like pure nastiness.

As I grew older, men molested me. The stories are too graphic to tell. I felt trapped and surrounded, and it blew my mind. I kept asking myself, *What's really going on here?*

I'd always go back to that hot tub of water. "Get this off me!" But you can't wash off the feeling or the scars; and at that age, you don't have the vocabulary to express what happened or the ability to go against adults and tell a responsible adult. Some of the people who molested me were religious.

These people were probably carrying sexual limps from their childhood only to pass them on to me.

The molestation I experienced set up limps in my life. The confusion it created in my life set me on the wrong course. I'm not making excuses because excuses will get me nowhere. We must deal with our sexuality where we are, trusting God for help with the good and the bad. It is foolish and unhealthy not to inventory your sexual past. Like any other part of your life, every interaction with a person, good or bad, influences you for better or worse.

By the time I was 11 or 12, I had lost all sexual sensitivity. All the boundaries had been ripped down. *If this is the way it is,* I told myself, *then at least I'm going to control it rather than have others control me!* I decided to try to sleep with every girl I could. Promiscuity consumed me.

I had given myself over to an all-too-common destructive way of life, and it became habitual. It felt good amid those few, brief sexual moments, but it totally controlled my thoughts. My thoughts became

> GOD'S PEOPLE WON'T KNOW COMPLETE VICTORY UNTIL WE ADDRESS OUR SEXUAL LIMPS, INDIVIDUALLY AND COLLECTIVELY, BECAUSE THERE IS NOT ANOTHER SIN THAT CAUSES US MORE INNER SHAME AND BONDAGE.

my actions. My actions became my character. That is the same pattern we all follow in any part of our life, good or bad.

Yet, it didn't take the dirty feeling away.

Instead, it sowed seeds of long-term destruction in me as well as in others around me. I've had to deal with the guilt of knowing that there are people who are probably still dealing with their sexual limps because of me because I didn't know how to deal with my own sexual limps.

Satan uses our sexual limps to beat us down so we limp worse than ever before. And I am convinced that God's people won't know complete victory until we address our sexual limps, individually and collectively, because there is not another sin that causes us more inner shame and bondage. That shame drags us into the gutter of our minds and hearts and separates us from other believers. There is no other sin that we try so badly to hide. It is the secret we keep to ourselves, and it eats us alive.

The church hasn't always talked honestly and often enough about sexual limps. We tend to avoid or brush over the most explosive, destructive area of our being: sexual immorality. It is highly probable that we are all sexually crippled in some way. Sexual issues are too complicated for any of us to have it all figured out because they are far more than physical. The more we ignore them, the worse our issues become. Silence defeats and cripples us. We just can't afford to remain silent anymore.

What Is a Sexual Limp?

Within the pages of this book, you won't find justifications or excuses for any sexual sins. That's not why I'm writing this. Fornication, adultery, lust—the Bible is clear, and I must be, too. All sexual sins are equally wrong.

Neither am I out to attack any group. The sin of homosexuality is no worse than the sin of adultery or fornication. All are sexual sins. The church shouldn't only highlight the sin of homosexuality but should also call out the sins of fornication and adultery, too, in addition to the plethora of other gaudy sexual sins.

How can we condone adultery or fornication and yet condemn homosexuality? We tend to "rate" one sexual sin as being worse than others thus deceiving ourselves into believing that we can linger in our self-defined, "lower-rated sins" and demonize those who commit the "higher-rated sins."

The mention of any sin is meant to stir repentance in the hearts of those who sin so that they will submit to following the Word of God. As the Bible says, we need to remove the plank out of our own eyes before trying to move the speck of sawdust out of the eyes of others (Matthew 7:3-5). So, we all are expected to recognize our sinfulness and repent.

Sexual sin is any sexual behavior outside the will of God as defined by His Word. Sexual sin is not based on how you feel about wounds in your past or about others' actions that have affected you sexually. There is a difference between sexual sins and sexual limps.

SEXUAL LIMPS

A sexual limp is the sum of the debilitating issues in your life that have caused, or are currently causing, you to struggle with maintaining a God-honoring sex life. You may not struggle with this every day, and the intensity of these emotions, feelings, or memories may come and go; but your past life and experiences feed into your current temptations or sin. They affect how you see yourself and your spouse. They affect how you look for a marriage partner.

As you're reflecting on your sexual limps, view them in context of fallen humanity. From the original sin of Adam and Eve, humanity developed a limp. So, just being a human being in a fallen world is a limp. If Jesus limped at all, it was because He put on human flesh. The reality is, however, that Jesus' incarnation was a demonstration of humility and love.

While our limps may result from our sin or someone else's, the Bible makes it clear that while Jesus identified with us firsthand, He Himself was without sin (1 Peter 2:22). Hebrews 4:15 also makes this clear: "For we do not have a high priest who is unable to empathize with our weaknesses, but we have one who has been tempted in every way, just as we are—yet he did not sin."

We are born in sin and shaped in iniquity. Our desires, which were God-given and natural from our beginning in the garden of Eden, have been perverted. Sex, after the need for food, is the greatest desire of the human body. As we mature, our bodies crave sex. With few exceptions, it's a natural part of who we are, and it is something we live with and must always deal with. So our sexual history, coupled with rampant, fallen desires, make up our sexual limps.

A Church of Sexual Cripples

According to Scripture, the Corinthian church was plagued with sexual immorality issues and had a high tolerance for sexually immorality (1 Corinthians 5–7). Their allowance of such practices may have stemmed from their pagan backgrounds. But this Corinthian church had gone even further than the pagans. The Corinthian church was admonished by Paul to stop tolerating a sexually immoral brother who was sleeping with or sexually involved with his father's wife (1 Corinthians 5:1-13). Paul continues in Chapters 6 and 7 to expound on how believers should live sexually moral lives.

Think about the church today. Even before we were born, the global culture has not only tolerated sexual immorality but keeps adding to what is considered tolerable or acceptable. Unfortunately, believers, yielding to their own flesh and limited thinking, also tolerate sexual immorality by their rationalization of it, their involvement in it, and their silence about it.

Are we exempt from obeying the Word of God because we limp sexually? Christ did not come for perfect people; He came for sinners. But in no way does He teach us to remain sinners, nor does He excuse us to continue in sin simply because we say, "I am saved, but I am struggling." No, we are to grow more and more into God's image. This is called sanctification.

Like the adulterous woman Jesus forgave, we are told to go and sin no more (John 8:11). Our sexual sins are covered by the blood of Jesus, but unless we do battle against these areas of sin in our lives, the devil can still defeat us. God has given us Himself in Christ and in the Holy Spirit. He gives us ways to escape (1 Corinthians 10:13), if we would only obey Him, the God we say we love (John 14:15).

When Paul wrote to the church at Corinth, he bluntly addressed the real issues they were experiencing. He wanted to make sure they did not misunderstand what was at stake.

We can see that the Corinthian believers were no different than we are today, and there are several lessons we can learn from what Paul taught them about sexual sins.

Our sexuality is out of line if it controls us instead of us controlling it. Paul said, "I will not be mastered by anything" (1 Corinthians 6:12). If you are limping in any area, it means at times that you have allowed that area to dominate your mind and body.

Our bodies are not our own, but they are God's, who designed it for purity and for good sexual relationships. "The body . . . is not meant for sexual immorality but for the Lord," Paul said (1 Corinthians 6:13). We may think our bodies are ours to do with as we want, but that isn't true. In fact, this passage says that our bodies are made "for the Lord, and the Lord for the body" (1 Corinthians 6:13). Our bodies are members of Christ. We are a living temple of God (1 Corinthians 6:19). How can we take Christ's presence into our sinful sexual practices?

Many people have adopted the mantra "If it feels good, do it." Others justify their behavior by using the excuse "I can't help myself." The good news is that through Christ we can (1 Corinthians 10:13).

In Christ, we have the power to be freed from the bondage of sexual sins and limps. Jesus conquered not just a few sins but all sins. Paul said, "By his power God raised the Lord from the dead, and he will raise us also" (1 Corinthians 6:14). When Christ saved you and filled you with the Holy Spirit, he saved you fully—mind, body, and spirit—giving you the ability to live in the Spirit and not gratify the lusts of the flesh.

Sexual Immorality

I met Maria in 1997. Maria's mother was 14 when she had Maria—a baby having a baby. Her mother didn't understand sex, so how could Maria understand it? When Maria was four, her mother's boyfriend began sexually abusing her.

The abuse continued for the next six years. Finally, Maria mustered up the courage to tell her mother, but her mother brushed it off as harmless playing. Maria insisted that what her mother's boyfriend was doing was wrong, but the abuse didn't stop.

Maria started to believe that abuse must just be the way life is supposed to be—ugly and demeaning and normal. She had been exposed to a sexually deviant adult. She tried to stand up to the predator, but he threatened to kill her mother if she did.

By the time she was a teenager, Maria had been gutted of God's beautiful sexual plan for her. She lost interest in men, who had only abused her. Her wounds went deep, which made her limp sexually. God's design for heterosexual maturity in her had been stunted, so she saw the girls around her as "safe." It was a strange tug: They were pretty and not predatory, and that felt appealing.

> IN CHRIST, WE HAVE THE POWER TO BE FREED FROM THE BONDAGE OF SEXUAL SINS AND LIMPS. JESUS CONQUERED NOT JUST A FEW SINS BUT ALL SINS.

Still, Maria tried to follow the traditional path. She married a good man, but her desires for women only intensified. She did not hide this from her husband because she did not want to be that way. He was amazingly understanding, praying with and encouraging her.

But armed robbers shot and killed her husband. At 27, Maria was shocked and alone. Soon after the death of her husband, she met a car mechanic who showed an interest in her. After spending time with this person, Maria suddenly realized that the mechanic was a woman who chose to live like a man. But she was so understanding and safe that Maria let herself be drawn into a relationship with her.

Maria was in search of peace, joy, and safety, as we all are. Her traditional church wasn't helping matters much. All she heard there every Sunday was the same old "get saved" sermon. Her spirit wanted more. She needed to hear preaching about all of life, including sex, money, lust, and greed and taking responsibility for her life.

Just because you are in sexual sin doesn't mean you aren't longing for what Christ can offer. If anything, it probably means that that's exactly what you want. You want true love, true joy, true pleasure, because you've been looking for love in all the wrong places, as the song goes. You are following the wrong path.

One day, Maria walked around the block from her old church to my church, New Jerusalem. She had been in a lesbian relationship for two years, but when she entered New Jerusalem, she was immediately blessed. She was greeted warmly, and she felt a sense of belonging. Eventually, she chose to obey Christ and ended her lesbian relationship. Maria even joined the choir, sharing her God-given talent of singing praises to God.

No Room for Rejection

Some people may wonder what draws sinners of any sort to churches. What is it about a particular church that makes people want to stay? No matter what our backgrounds are, Christ is the one who draws us. Before knowing Christ, we were all sinners who needed Jesus and a body of people who would love us.

Knowing how God's love drew us, why then do we struggle loving sexually immoral people? We have all been in some category of immorality or many categories with sexual immorality being most likely included on the list rather in thought or deed.

Maybe one of the reasons we struggle so much with receiving sexually immoral people into a place where they can get the help they need is because we haven't adequately addressed our own sexual sins. Satan has deceived us into justifying and excusing our sexual sins by believing that because they are of a certain type then somehow they don't count.

Satan tries to convince us that we're either too dirty to go to church or that once we go, we won't be received. We assume that people will somehow know everything about us and, subsequently, will reject us. Even amid assumptions and fears about being accepted, God is still at work and readies a group of believers to receive us with the gospel message of love and discipleship.

> TO BE HEALED, YOU NEED TO MOVE TOWARD CHRIST, NOT AWAY FROM HIM, AND YOU CAN'T BE DISTRACTED BY THOSE WHO MIGHT PROCLAIM YOU TOO DIRTY TO BE HEALED.

When Maria walked into New Jerusalem, one of our dearest members walked right up to her and hugged her. When I met her, Maria was thinking, *Doesn't this pastor see the dirt on me?* But at the time, we didn't know her sexual history, and it shouldn't have mattered even if we did. When we greet visitors into our churches, we just never know how badly they might need that hug, smile, or warm hello.

To be healed, you need to move toward Christ, not away from Him, and you can't be distracted by those who might proclaim you too dirty to be healed. Everyone may not accept you, but God will lead you to people of mercy. Jesus is our Shepherd, and He has a place for us to be received despite our sinful condition.

Our churches must bear responsibility, too. We are under a massive attack by Satan because he wants to keep the people of God impure and degraded. His plans are realized when someone else sins against you sexually and then when you sin against someone else sexually. Then he deceives you into justifying your sexual sin by finding someone else like

Maria to point to as sexually worse than you are. It is a cycle of sexual dysfunction in which Satan wants to trap us.

We can't afford to keep feeding this cycle. Instead of pointing fingers and comparing whose sins are worse, we need to reach out to those in sexual entrapments and help them to know that freedom or deliverance is available, as it is with any sin. When we learn to submit fully to the way of Chris, we all can be set free.

We only multiply our sexual frustration when we try to solve our issues outside of Christ or when we try to point fingers at others and not ourselves. Sexually immorality, like all sin, cannot be rationalized. When we attempt to rationalize it anyway, we often just pile more dysfunction on top of our sexual dysfunction.

But as bad as our sexual limps may be, I worry that it will only get worse for future generations. Our society is on a downward spiral, and dealing with sexual limps and attitudes is vital to the future welfare of our children. If you can't find the courage to work on your limps for your own well-being, perhaps you should think of doing so for the future of your children. If your children were playing in the middle of the road, and a car was speeding in their direction, wouldn't you risk your life to save them? Sexual immorality is that speeding car, so save your children.

We must break the cycle of sexual dysfunction simultaneously amongst believers and in our world, in our country, in our communities, in our churches, in our families, and in our homes. We are without excuse. To fight this epidemic, we must adopt the strategic warfare prescribed in Scripture. The Bible says to "flee from sexual immorality" (1 Corinthians 6:18). In the Amplified Bible, 1 Corinthians 6:18 reads, "Run away from sexual immorality [in any form, whether thought or behavior, whether visual or written]." The Lord tells us to flee or to run away because we just can't trust ourselves, our flesh.

Three-Pronged Attack

Satan has a three-pronged attack against us: the lust of the flesh, the lust of the eye, and the pride of life (1 John 2:15-17). To successfully fight the enemy, we need to dig deeper and explore each of these weapons.

The lust of the flesh. Satan wants to pervert your body's natural desires. Physical hunger is natural, but overeating can be harmful to our bodies. Satan often uses sex in the same way. He encourages us to overindulge or to indulge outside of God's design, thus making us sexual gluttons.

Satan distorts the purpose for which we were created. We were not meant to have multiple sex partners. Just as God made Adam and Eve for each other, God made you for somebody in the covenant of marriage. That might sound unbelievable given how contemporary culture promotes a casual approach to sex and encourages us to have as many sexual partners as we want. Many of us have been led astray from God's divine design for sex by what society bombards us with every day.

Today, we often bring multiple past sexual experiences into our marriages. Such a past can cause great pain and displeasure sexually.

I know this from personal experience.

Tracy and I had had totally opposite sexual experiences. She hadn't been with anyone but me, while I had been with so many. So, needless to say, there were some challenges when we first got married. My appetite for sex had to be tamed. It was unfair and unrealistic for me to expect my wife to live up to what I was used to in a promiscuous lifestyle.

The lust of the eye. Satan tries to distort your vision. It's not only about what you see, but it's how you see it. When you look at a person, how do you look at him or her? Do you imagine yourself with the person? Do you undress the person with your eyes? If so, you sin against the person and against your spouse (or your future spouse).

Think about how you interact with the opposite sex. Do you try to arouse them when you come in contact with them? Do you use sex as a weapon to advance at work or in life? Are you guilty of using sex appeal to manipulate others? We should all aim to be like Job, who said, "I have made a covenant with my eyes; how then could I gaze at a virgin?" (Job 31:1, NAS).

Another area to be vigilant against is the media—movies, TV shows, Internet sites—that we're exposed to almost every day. Proverbs 21:4 says, "Haughty eyes and a proud heart—the unplowed field of the wicked—produce sin." Many of the things we watch have the potential to cause us to lust; and once we consume certain visual images, they are recorded in our memories and retrieved at will because of our own lust and desires.

Jesus knew about the power of the eyes: "Your eye is the lamp of your body. When your eyes are healthy, your whole body also is full of light. But when they are unhealthy, your body also is full of darkness" (Luke 11:34). Jesus says in Luke 11:35, "See to it, then, that the light within you is not darkness."

There is hope, but we have to make an agreement, or a covenant, with our eyes. Perhaps it's easier said than done, but we have to agree not to look where we shouldn't look, not to open our vision or our imagination to those images that will cripple or destroy us sexually. Honoring this covenant will be difficult and, at times, will seem impossible to keep. But it is more than doable through Christ, who has given us the indwelling of the Holy Spirit.

Today, the real danger is that Satan is using the abundance of sexual images to infiltrate the minds of current and future generations, which may cause them to have sexual limps, too. Are sexual limps inevitable for everyone? Maybe not, but they are definitely highly probable for most.

Before you tell yourself that's not true, think about the movies or television shows you may have watched with your children. When we allow our children to watch a movie filled with sexually teasing scenes, even if we tell them to close their eyes during those scenes while we continue to watch because we're adults who think that we can handle it, then we're contributing to the problem. We're being hypocritical.

When we give our children smartphones, we may be subjecting them to things we ourselves cannot even handle. I'm not saying children can't have smartphones, and I understand why parents give them to their children. But I am saying that we can't just hand those phones over to our children without first teaching them how to avoid the dangers they might encounter and without monitoring their activity.

As you can see, when dealing with the lust of the eyes, not only are we responsible for guarding our own eyes, but we must take responsibility for shielding the eyes of our children. If the eyes are the window to the soul, we've already let in too many images that are detrimental to the happiness and well-being of ourselves and our families. But through Christ, we can cleanse the eyes of our spirits and start anew.

> WE'VE ALREADY LET IN TOO MANY IMAGES THAT ARE DETRIMENTAL TO THE HAPPINESS AND WELL-BEING OF OURSELVES AND OUR FAMILIES. BUT THROUGH CHRIST, WE CAN CLEANSE THE EYES OF OUR SPIRITS AND START ANEW.

The pride of life. Satan deceives us into trying to justify our bad behavior. We tell ourselves, "My sex drive is just too powerful, and my spouse can't ever fulfill my needs." "I can't help it if the ladies throw themselves at me!" or "It's not my fault that this guy is so attracted to me and keeps pushing me to have sex!"

Behind each of these excuses is a well of false pride. We've convinced ourselves that biology makes us do what we do and we're powerless against it or that we're just so attractive that our casual approach to sex must be all right. Sometimes we even cover our deception with a sheen of spirituality: "These kinds of sexual viewing habits on TV or the movies would hurt some other people I know, but thank God I'm more mature and above that kind of temptation."

All lies!

When we live in denial about our sinfulness and refuse to own up to what we have done or what we do, we give the enemy an upper hand in our lives.

Once you've submerged yourself deep in sexual sin, initially, your pride makes you believe you can hide it. You rationalize and justify your behavior, hiding behind a variety of excuses. You also think you're just clever enough to live two lifestyles—one in the light and one in the darkness of sexual sin. You believe you're fooling everyone, and you may be for a while, but eventually your secret is uncovered.

So, don't be fooled. Even a child can hide his or her sin for a little while. But the longer things play out, the more callous and numb your own senses become to the harmfulness and darkness of your sexual sin. Before you know it, your conscience has become seared, and you begin to believe that your actions are acceptable. This is the worst kind of pride.

By now, as a believer, you are ignoring the Holy Spirit in your life. Romans 1:24-27 has some scary things to say about people who live like this. Basically, your natural desires become corrupted, wherein you are subject to shameful lusts.

Don't be discouraged by this passage, but know that we can never fool God with our lies. There is no closet so deep or so dark that we can hide in that will conceal from Him what we've done or even what we've been thinking about doing.

To let go of your pride and come out from your hiding place will require you to be honest with yourself and with God. Tell yourself that you are going to stop hiding because despite how clever you think you've been, if you've had to hide your sins, then everything is not all right in your life.

Perhaps you've told yourself so many times that what you're doing is all right to the point where you believe it, but that still doesn't make it right. You're just in denial. Whatever your sexual sin, let go of your pride and repent.

No Overnight Successes

Working through your sexual problems won't happen overnight. There is a path you will need to follow, which will lead to healing progress with your limps. So, now is the time to get out your map (your Bible) and prayerfully get back on the right path. God will lead you there.

Act Now

Sexual immorality is like sitting in a wind tunnel. Inside that tunnel you can't move forward, and with every attempt to do so you just exhaust yourself as you're pushed farther backward until you hit a wall and knock yourself out. But you need to act now and pursue the truth.

If you are dating someone and you are having sex, together with your girlfriend or boyfriend, *confess your sin to a responsible party—* a pastor or a marriage counselor. Seek prayer and advice. Covenant with your future spouse to remain pure until marriage from this point forward. It's never too late to adopt a lifestyle of purity, and God will bless your efforts to remain pure until marriage. Victory is victory, and this will translate into your future life together.

If you are living with someone, *go to your pastor and begin discussing marriage.* Perhaps you've been

> SEXUAL IMMORALITY IS LIKE SITTING IN A WIND TUNNEL. INSIDE THAT TUNNEL YOU CAN'T MOVE FOREWARD, AND WITH EVERY ATTEMPT TO DO SO YOU JUST EXHAUST YOURSELF.

telling yourself and other people that you will eventually get married at some vague future time. But instead of procrastinating, waiting for a "perfect" time to get married, go to your pastor and put the wheels in motion. If you didn't already know, there will never be a perfect time, so take a positive step and get married.

If you have children, *talk to them about the beauty of sex*. Instead of letting the schools frame the discussion long before your children are ready, pray and ask God to give you wisdom to know when and how to discuss sex with them. In the meantime, help them to guard their hearts and minds against perverted images and the world's casual approach to sex and intimacy. If you need help, consult your pastor or Christian family counselor for recommendations on good books that will give you more information.

If you have older children, *talk to them about the mistakes you made and the consequences of your actions*. Don't try to hide your mistakes or pretend you've been perfect all your life. You are the most powerful influence for your children, and what you say carries a lot of weight. Sometimes the best way to reach our children is to honestly explain to them how certain sexual sins and lifestyle choices hurt and scarred us. When you talk to them, you may find that they will trust you enough to open up to you about their own previous mistakes. Praise God, and let the healing begin.

If you are struggling with a mind filled with sexual impurity, *pray and ask God to help you to repent*. Once you find yourself on the path to purity, *fill your mind with God's Word.* Don't make excuses or wallow in lust. When you read and digest God's Word, that leaves hardly any room for Satan to plant seeds of sexual sins. God's Word will also empower you to live an outward life of purity that will, in time, transform your inward life.

If you run across any bumps in the road to purity, *find a brother or a sister of the same sex to whom you can confess and to whom you can be accountable.* That person can pray for you and pick you up when you fall. Avoid isolation. Stop living in silence. Don't mistake a cry for help as weakness.

Above all, *don't give up on your goal of sexual purity.* God has made you for sexual purity, and He will honor you as you limp along your journey.

A Happy Ending

When Maria eventually told me she was living in a lesbian relationship, that was the start of her sexual healing. Neither the church nor I ostracized her. Rather, Maria has become one of the greatest examples of God's grace at work, and she has encouraged us.

Maria's honesty led her to real prayers of pain and repentance. She took the risk of entering a heterosexual dating relationship, but it failed, not because of her sexual sin but because of the other person's. It hurt her. She knew she had to hear from God, so she told Him, "I need some pain to be erased away because I am hurting!" And in time, God answered her prayers.

In 2000, Dan walked into Maria's life. He wanted to date her, but she admitted she was afraid and felt unworthy and unlovely. For years, Maria had been struggling with a physical condition that caused her to lose her hair. When Dan came by her house to visit, Maria's head was uncovered. She thought, *Surely, Dan will stop being interested in me if I open that door now!*

Maria opened the door, and Dan said, "Oh my God, you have got to be the most beautiful thing I've ever seen in my life!"

Then and there, Maria fell in love with Dan, and they began building a solid foundation of friendship. During the six years of building their friendship, God helped Maria rebuild her life. When Maria and Dan married and they finally made love, "it was the most beautiful thing," she gladly tells people.

Sex is no longer dirty to Maria, and it's no longer a secret. Now, sex is a source of joy and an expression of true love.

10. MENTAL LIMPS

"Peace I leave with you, my peace I give unto you: not as the world giveth, give I unto you. Let not your heart be troubled, neither let it be afraid." (John 14:27)

If you met Andrew, you might be surprised that he considers himself a loner. The 20-something-year-old is good-looking, a great teacher, and a committed mentor to junior-high students. Articulate and charming, he smoothly spins off witty one-liners. But Andrew has a mental limp that he's been dealing with since he was a child. Other people's life choices have negatively affected him and left him scarred. His parents divorced when he was just eight months old, leaving his mother to raise him and his siblings. His parents' divorce started Andrew on a spiral of insecurity, causing him to have abandonment and trust issues. Andrew rarely saw his father, and when he did, the outcome was often negative.

On his sixth birthday, Andrew asked his father for a birthday present. His father shot back, "Your child support check is your birthday present!" As a result, Andrew still has trouble asking for help or depending on other people.

When Andrew was a teenager, another man came into his mother's life, and Andrew decided to try to open up to him. They became close, but before long, things took a turn for the worse. One morning, Andrew's father picked him up from school and drove him home. When they arrived, Andrew saw yellow police tape encircling the house. His mother's boyfriend, the man Andrew had decided to trust, had stabbed her 19 times.

Just like Andrew, we try to escape our limps and find people we can trust and depend on. But in this fallen, sinful world, inevitably, reality hits us hard. Life hit Andrew hard and caused his mental limps. With everything that was happening to him in his young life, he developed a sense of distrust. His distrust caused him to create a wall of self-protection between him and everyone else.

Andrew began to keep other people at bay to prevent himself from being hurt. His mental blocks kept him from developing personal relationships. First, his father abandoned him. Then another man killed his mother. He vowed he wouldn't let anyone that close to him again.

All of us have been hurt at one time or another, which causes us to create mental blocks and put up walls between ourselves and other

> ALL OF US HAVE BEEN HURT AT ONE TIME OR ANOTHER, WHICH CAUSES US TO CREATE MENTAL BLOCKS AND PUT UP WALLS BETWEEN OURSELVES AND OTHER PEOPLE.

people. We allow the fear of our past to dictate how we treat people in our present; and when we leave those fears unaddressed, they cause us to stumble or to limp through life. They limit our progress as adults, parents, friends, professionals, and church members.

What Is a Mental Limp?

For the purpose of this book, I define *mental limps* as issues associated with a person's mindset or perspective. Usually, particular mindsets are developed early in life. If we've had negative events take place in our past, it becomes easy to develop a negative mindset as we move into adulthood. Our perspective becomes skewed, and we allow what happened to us to hinder our progress, to keep us from being successful, and stop us from moving at an appropriate pace into our destiny. It's like being stuck in a box. Regardless of how hard we try, we can't break through, which in turn causes us to stop trying. That's a mental limp.

It is highly probable that all other limps have a mental component. For example, if you limp sexually, that limp originated from a negative mindset that has manifested itself into a sexual limp. But God wants to free you of these mental limps that have a hold on you.

If your limps are oppressing you, it could mean that you have lost focus of God. By this I mean that if limps are holding you down in your life, then you probably aren't focusing on praising God and grasping His greatness. It is hard to move forward when you continue to focus on everything except God. God wants you to be free of mental limps so you can praise Him wholeheartedly.

When the prophet Isaiah pleaded his case to God, he knew that God wanted him whole so he could worship God. "In your love you kept me from the pit of destruction; you have put all my sins behind your back. For the grave cannot praise you, death cannot sing your praise. . . . The living, the living—they praise you, as I am doing today" (Isaiah 38:17-19).

God has given you the power to walk with limps, enabling you to rise above your mental limps. In no way am I suggesting that the issues that concern you are made up in your head; however, I am suggesting that you already possess what you need in order to rise above your current mindset. God is at work in your life even though you don't always recognize His presence.

The Source of Mental Limps

A bad mindset doesn't just spring from nowhere. Mental limps come from a deep source.

Whatever you believe about yourself, good or bad, comes from a mindset that was established by your past experiences and your interactions with other people. If you have accepted that others have the right to abuse you, it's because abuse may have been normal in your past. If you believe your ethnicity makes you inferior, that's because someone planted the seed of inferiority somewhere along the way.

Mindsets are not the source of your problems; they are the result of the source.

Artesian water wells produce clean, drinkable water. People who live in rural areas can locate them behind their houses or out in the woods. The water from those wells usually runs at about the same speed as water would from a faucet that you turn on with one twist. However, people who know about wells say that underneath that small stream of water is a massive underground lake called an aquifer. You may see the small stream springing from the well, but you never see the gigantic source.

In the same way, mental limps are like small, above-ground streams. They come from somewhere deep—an unseen mental aquifer. That aquifer is often full of pain and brokenness from our past. It is where we have learned and formed our mindsets, and it is where our mental limps are created.

Examples of Mental Limps

When people say, "I'll never get married again," that's an example of a mental limp. Perhaps they made that statement because of a bad previous marriage. Or perhaps it was due to how critical others were after their divorce. Maybe they're afraid of risk, or perhaps they lack faith. The aquifer of pain is there, and it pushes to the top the mental limps concerning commitment and marriage. As a result, they won't allow themselves to enter a serious relationship that could lead to marriage.

When people say, "I can never get promoted at work," that is a mental limp that originated from a negative mindset. Likely, this mindset came from the pain of past failures or from the destructive criticism of someone powerful such as a parent, a teacher, or another authority figure.

Another possible mental limp is when we compare ourselves with others. When we always believe that someone else has more or has something better than we do, we spend so much time worrying about measuring up to them that we never progress in developing our true selves. This limp also includes the shame we feel about our bodies as we compare how we look to how other people look.

Sometimes we spend so much time and money trying to change how we look to conform to some societal standard that we don't address the core issues of this mental limp. It's difficult to reach the place God wants us to reach when we compare ourselves to others in a negative way. Instead of trying to live up to some manmade, pseudo standard to please others, we should try to live to please God.

Another mental limp that works hand in hand with comparing ourselves to others is when we hide behind excuses. We reveal this particular limp when we look at what other people have and claim that what they have has given them certain advantages. We say that because we don't have what they have or didn't grow up like they did then we can't help that we aren't further along in life than we are. We excuse our behavior by blaming others for our misfortunes and unwise decisions, and nothing is ever our fault. While it's true that some of our mental limps are rooted in our past because of other people's actions, that does not give us a license to wallow in self-pity and excuse our current behavior.

The Grasshopper Mentality

The grasshopper mentality can keep us from reaching our divine destiny. We can see the impact of the grasshopper mentality on the journey of the children of Israel. The grasshopper mentality is a way of thinking that can hinder us all from time to time because it inhibits us from continuing to try or aim for better because of imaginary restrictions.

According to Numbers 13:21-32, the children of Israel exemplified the grasshopper mentality in full effect. They declared that they looked like grasshoppers in their own sight as well as in the sight of the other people in the land.

> WHILE IT'S TRUE THAT SOME OF OUR MENTAL LIMPS ARE ROOTED IN OUR PAST BECAUSE OF OTHER PEOPLE'S ACTIONS, THAT DOES NOT GIVE US A LICENSE TO WALLOW IN SELF-PITY AND EXCUSE OUR CURRENT BEHAVIOR.

After spying out the Promised Land, which was theirs for the taking, the spies said, "There we saw the giants . . . ; and *we were like grasshoppers in our own sight, and so we were in their sight* (Numbers 13:32, emphasis added)." With this statement, ten of the spies "gave the children of Israel a bad report" (Numbers 13:32). The spies' report caused the children of Israel to focus on their weaknesses instead of what they could accomplish through God, who had brought them to this point.

Having a grasshopper mentality makes you focus on your weaknesses instead of God's power within you. Once you've taken on this mentality, it takes prayer and acts of faith and trust in God to dispel it.

Unfortunately, negative news spreads much faster than good news. Among the Israelites, the spies' bad report spread fear and uncertainty. Although God had promised them the new land, they were afraid to claim it because of the negative report they had heard. Soon, they were mentally limping, and many of them missed entering the Promised Land. These were the same people who had seen God part the Red Sea, send manna from heaven, and give them water from a rock. Still, their grasshopper mentality filled them with doubt and fear.

Growing up in the Mississippi Delta, I loved to romp and roam with my friends, and we would often catch grasshoppers. The curious thing about grasshoppers is that if you put them in a box with holes punched in it and close the lid, they will keep hopping.

You can hear the grasshoppers hitting their heads as they try to escape. They wear themselves down as they bang their heads on the box lid. When you finally open the box, the grasshoppers won't jump out because they've hit their heads so many times that when they get the chance to break free, they are conditioned not to jump but to stay put.

We are the same way when we take on a grasshopper mentality. We try in our own strength to break out of a situation. We exert all of the emotional and physical energy we can muster. But if God is not in it or it is not God's timing, then it is just like we are banging our heads against the top of a closed boxed. It wears us down so much so that we stop trying to break free. We lose the vision for overcoming our obstacles and achieving our dreams.

Then when God lifts the lid on the box and it's time for us to jump to freedom, we won't. We've worn ourselves down, we've lost our faith and courage, and we've accepted the box as our new normal.

In God's timing, the children of Israel were being called to conquer the giants standing in the way of achieving their dreams. Instead of pursuing their enemies with faith in God, they complained and whined about how big their enemies were and how they couldn't possibly conquer them. God was lifting the lid off the box and telling them to jump to freedom, but they didn't jump. Instead, they grumbled. God forgave them at Moses' request; however, He declared that none of those who had witnessed how He had delivered them from Egypt would enter the Promised Land (Numbers 14:1-36).

The Israelites had a great dream of entering the Promised Land. For 400 years, they had dreamed that they might find a fruitful place they could call their own. When Moses delivered them by God's power, their dreams of reaching the Promised Land swelled. Their faith rose. But when it came time for them to act in faith, they didn't. Their mental limps hindered them. They had become mental grasshoppers, and they missed the blessing of entering the land.

> WE'VE OFTEN SPENT DECADES SUFFERING UNDER THE CRIPPLING CIRCUMSTANCES THAT HAVE RESULTED FROM BAD INFLUENCES, ACTIONS, AND DECISIONS. WE HAVE BEEN CAUGHT IN OUR OWN "EGYPT."

Your Promised Land

We all have a "promised land." It may not be a place, but it may be a goal. Whatever form it takes, this promised land was put in your heart by God. It is the destination and dreams God has given you. But the one condition God has placed on you before receiving this promised land is that you must act in obedience when He calls.

We may dream of getting out of debt. However, when God directs us to get a second job to give us the extra income to pay down our debt, we limp away from our promised land rather than act in faith. Some of us may want to go to college. We allow the grasshopper mentality to make us feel inadequate, and we cower in fear.

God may be calling us to move into a promised land of new friendships and relationships with people who will build us up, not tear us down. However, Satan whispers in our ears that our old friends may be bad in some ways, but on the "positive side," they are comfortably predictable. So, we remain with them rather than risk the unknown and make new friends.

Our mental limps have been forged in the many years of mental slavery we've endured. Like the children of Israel, we've often spent decades suffering under the crippling circumstances that have resulted from bad influences, actions, and decisions. We have been caught in our own "Egypt." The words *positive change* probably never entered the Israelites vocabulary, but that doesn't have to be the case for us.

Change requires effort, prayer, and faith. To start positive change, you have to repent of sinful patterns. Repentance isn't popular today, but it is mandatory. You have to make a 180-degree turn in how you think about yourself and your challenges. No more grasshopper mentality.

Next, you have to call out your mental limps for what they are: mental limps that came from a negative mindset.

You can't fool God, and you really can't fool most people like you think; so, don't try to sugarcoat your situation. If you want to change, you have to acknowledge where you are—where you really are. The best way to do that is to address your negative mental traits and the obstacles they've caused. Consider these examples.

The strength of other people. The Israelites said that the inhabitants of the Promised Land were stronger than they were. Strength and power can be intimidating, whether it is physical, financial, verbal, or emotional. We often seek strength in all the wrong places and are disappointed when we find we're unable to conquer our problems. God wants to be our strength. We have to lose our mental limps that cause us to believe that all the power we need is inside of us.

In encouraging Paul through his weaknesses, God told him, "My grace is sufficient for you, for my power is made perfect in weakness." Then Paul could say, "Therefore I will boast all the more gladly about my weaknesses, so that Christ's power may rest on me" (2 Corinthians 12:9). Joshua and Caleb understood this same principle. As tough as they were, it was God's power that would conquer the Promised Land for the Israelites, not theirs. And it's God's power that will conquer your promised land, too.

The size of the walls. The Israelites whined that "the cities [were] fortified and very large" (Numbers 13:28). They had no vision for clearing these walls through God's strength. We also doubt God's strength to help us through difficult situations. We say we can't go back to school, get a promotion, or get married. But God says, "They will soar on wings like eagles; they will run and not grow weary, they will walk and not be faint" (Isaiah 40:31). With eagles' wings, you can soar over the walls in your life and not even feel tired.

The size of people and issues. The children of Israel said, "We even saw the descendants of Anak [who came from giants]" (Numbers 13:28). I have to admit that I would find a giant to be intimidating. Seeing real giants in our promised land might cause us to doubt if we can enter, but we can't dwell in fear and doubt. The size of the people or issues in life can't dictate how we live. If we surrender to how big things are, we will never reach our promised land.

Giants are just another obstacle, and God has experience when it comes to slaying giants. When our blood pressure is up and the adrenaline of fear is rushing through us, we forget to stand on the truth of God's Word and on the great deeds He has already done for us and for others. When facing giants, we need to do as David did before he faced Goliath. He recalled to himself and others the time God allowed him to kill a bear and a lion. That gave him faith to face an even greater obstacle. We must be aware of these factors and be prepared to do battle with them. They can only defeat us if we walk in our flesh rather than filling our hearts and minds with God's Spirit.

Caleb and Joshua saw the giants living in the Promised Land. They believed they could conquer them with God's help and eventually they took them out, and so can you.

A Giant-Slaying Mentality

You can be a giant-slayer. You can be a Caleb or a Joshua, two men who rose up against the bad report of the other ten spies. Unlike the others, their minds and emotions led them to fresh faith. Their words and actions revealed a giant-slaying mentality that you too can access by God's Spirit. When you do, you will see your mental limps heal. Consider what Joshua and Caleb did.

Joshua and Caleb believed God's promises. It was enough that God had promised them the land. Even if their minds told them that the obstacles were too great, they did not waver. For these two men, God had promised it, so they were going for it! God has made promises to us, too. He has promised us peace (John 14:27), rest (Matthew 11:28), and renewed strength (Isaiah 40:29, 31). God makes us conquerors through His love (Romans 8:37), and He makes good plans for us (Jeremiah 29:11).

When Joshua and Caleb heard the other spies' bad report, they reacted immediately and decisively to block it from their spirits. Numbers 14:6 says that they tore their clothes when they heard the children of Israel complaining and showing a lack of faith.

Overcoming mental limps requires decisive action. Block out any bad reports and the negativity that kills faith. Ultimately, you are fighting spiritual warfare, and you must stand tall and strong and act decisively just as Joshua and Caleb did. You must make battlefield decisions: "Be strong in the Lord and in his mighty power. Put on the full armor of God, so that you can take your stand against the devil's schemes" (Ephesians 6:10-11). Stand against the bad reports that Satan keeps feeding your mind.

In the ancient Near East, the tearing of one's clothes was a visible sign of repentance and remorse. Instead of saying, "Amen," which means "may it be," tearing one's clothes was like saying, "No! May this never be!"

So when Joshua and Caleb heard the bad report and tore their clothes, they were speaking to their own minds, saying, "May it never be! We won't listen to this old mindset any more. We are turning and trusting God for great things." When we "tear our clothes," we are saying, "No! I will not receive the bad report. I will not allow any negativity to keep me from God's promises."

> OVERCOMING MENTAL LIMPS REQUIRES DECISIVE ACTION. BLOCK OUT ANY BAD REPORTS AND THE NEGATIVITY THAT KILLS FAITH.

These two giant-slayers spoke words of faith. In Numbers 13:30, Caleb says, "We should go up and take possession of the land, for we can certainly do it." One of the vital ways to fight a mental limp is to begin to speak words of faith out loud against it. Confess out loud to yourself and others what you are believing God will do for you.

First Timothy 6:12 tells us that we are to "fight the good fight of faith." The way we do that is to "take hold of the eternal life to which [we] were called when [we] made [our] *good confession in the presence of many witnesses*" (emphasis added).

When we confess with our mouths, we move from mental limping to giant-slaying. We are in a fight against a bigger enemy than mortal giants. Confessing God's Word and promises are effective strategies in our arsenal of faith.

Joshua and Caleb stepped out in faith because they knew God was with them. They told the other Israelites, "The LORD is with us" (Numbers 14:9). God is with us, too. That fact was fully realized in the coming of Christ, Immanuel, and His sending of the Holy Spirit to reside in our lives.

We now have God's full presence with us in an even greater way than Joshua and Caleb did. God is here right now to remove that mental limp of yours. Once you realize that you are constantly in His presence, this should change your mindset. After all, "If God is for us, who can be against us?" (Romans 8:31).

They reminded themselves of the real prize ahead. In Numbers 14:7-8, they said, "The land . . . is exceedingly good, . . . a land flowing with milk and honey." What is your dream? What is your promised land? Keep your eyes focused on it no matter what obstacles you encounter.

Don't let the obstacles block your vision, and don't allow the giants to intimidate you. When you are fearful or tired, remind yourself of the great prize that God has awaiting you. By keeping the proper focus and reminding yourself of what is to come, you can see beyond the giants. You can find new strength to overcome.

Paul wrote the Corinthians to remind them of the gospel message, even though they were already believers. He urged them to keep pursuing the ultimate prize: their salvation. "Brothers and sisters, I want to remind you of the gospel I preached to you, which you received and on which you have taken your stand. By this gospel you are saved, if you hold firmly to the word I preached to you" (1 Corinthians 15:1-2).

Joshua and Caleb replaced their fear with confidence. They said, "Only do not rebel against the LORD. And do not be afraid of the people of the land, because we will devour them" (Numbers 14:9). These two giant-slayers were ready to rumble because they were too close to reaching their dream.

You may be closer to realizing your promised land than you think. It may be just around the corner in your life, but you will never know if you accept your mental limp. Get up and replace your old mentality of fear with a new mindset of confidence.

As they took steps of faith and spoke words of faith, the power of God in the midst of Joshua and Caleb wiped out the fear that any mental limp had bred in them. Jesus set the matter of fear into context. He said that we should not fear people who can only hurt us physically. "Do not be afraid of those who kill the body but cannot kill the soul. Rather, be afraid of the One who can destroy both soul and body in hell" (Matthew 10:28).

How It All Comes Together

So what does it look like when we overcome a mental limp? Instead of looking like a mere snapshot of our lives, it more resembles a TV series that we watch unfold over a long period of time.

Gradually, God moves you from a grasshopper mentality to a giant-slayer mentality. Turning off that faucet of mental negativity that comes from a massive aquifer isn't always a one-time thing. Often, the faucet insists on dripping. We turn it off again. It drips again, but finally it is sealed.

When we experience healing from mental limps, we inspire others. Someday, someone will see us walking in faith amid a trial, and they will be inspired to begin the process of overcoming their mental limp. That's how it has been unfolding for Andrew. He has been winning the battle against his mental limps, and now God is using him to help others in their battles. It took Andrew acting in decisive faith against great giants.

When Andrew's family gathered at his father's house on the day of his mother's death, he sneaked outside to be alone. He could hear the conversation and crying going on inside.

More than anything else, people were saying, "What's going to happen to Drew now? What's Drew going to do?"

At that point, Andrew knew what he had to do. He stopped crying, and he walked back into the house. "An amazing breath of strength came over me, and I haven't cried since that day." It was as if, mentally and spiritually, Andrew resolved, like Joshua or Caleb, to make it in life. He would enter into his promised land. It would not be easy, but with God's help, he could do it.

Then the giants seemed to rise up immediately in Andrew's life. He was surprised a few days after his mother's death when his father signed over guardianship of Andrew to his sister, who already had a daughter. It hurt him deeply. But with his sister's help, his grades improved and so did his walk with God. They found a new church where they could grow. Eventually, Andrew graduated cum laude from Jackson State University.

All along, Andrew has been fighting giants. He has limped mentally, but over time, his gait has grown stronger. Today, he has a vision for teaching and guiding other children enduring those pivotal junior-high years. He teaches at a middle school in Jackson where God has given him a special ability to connect with youth who need the very sort of instruction he so hungered for at their age.

All of that time that Andrew was wandering in the wilderness of pain, God was making him strong. God has now put a dream into his heart and mind of helping children reach their potential. "They can relate to me," he says. He writes Bible verses on his dry-erase board, and this gives his students a chance to talk about life together.

Andrew hasn't missed a day of work in over three years of teaching. He even goes to the mall on Saturdays so his students can see him there. This past May marked the tenth anniversary of his mother's death, when his greatest mental limp was inflicted. But today, God uses this overcomer to do great things that would make his mother proud.

The answer to mental limps is not simple. Andrew is still struggling with his past, but recently he took the stage of New Jerusalem Church with me and told his story for the first time. As he spoke, you could sense God at work not only in his life but also in the lives of those listening. God is healing Andrew because he is acting in faith, and God will do the same for you.

11. PHYSICAL LIMPS

"Who shall separate us from the love of Christ? Shall trouble or hardship or persecution or famine or nakedness or danger or sword? . . . In all these things we are more than conquerors through him who loved us"
(Romans 8:35, 37).

Vic has two physical limps that started long ago. Before he acquired those limps, he seemed to be on top of the world. His parents were well-to-do; they owned restaurants and bars throughout the Jackson, Mississippi area. So, Vic was speeding through life on cruise control.

But at 14, Vic started drinking, and by 15, he was doing drugs. Even though he was raised in the church, he soon abandoned it. No one, including Vic, foresaw how bad things were going to get.

In college, Vic majored in finance and minored in marketing. Drug addiction, however, dug its hooks into his life. Still, as Vic entered the workforce, he appeared to his coworkers to be together. He made good money in a good career field. He owned condos, houses, and motorcycles, and he was a captain in the army.

Inwardly, however, Vic was withering. He was alienating his wife and children. Drugs had secretly become his master—a limp that Satan was using to destroy him, and it wasn't long before he found himself in prison. "I had walked away from God," he said before our congregation. He lost everything to the two-headed monster of addiction and incarceration.

Addiction and Incarceration

I'm not diminishing physical limps such as sickness, injury, or other afflictions. More lives today, however, are being destroyed by addiction and incarceration than we can fathom.

> ADDICTIONS HAPPEN BECAUSE WE HAVE UNSATISFIED HOLES IN OUR LIVES, AND WE USE THEM TO TRY TO SATISFY OURSELVES INSTEAD OF RELYING ON JESUS.

I once had on my staff an employee who was a recovering addict. He seemed healed, but he made the mistake of driving by his old haunt, a drug den. Before long, he fell back into his perverse lifestyle. A friend and I had to drag him out of that place. Fortunately, he's clean now and back on the road to recovery.

I asked him, "Why did you return to that deadly lifestyle?"

"Pastor," he said, "I was riding down the road, and I passed by a place where I used to do crack. With no intention of doing it, I passed by the place, then I went on home. But every day after that, I could hear crack calling my name."

Are physical addictions calling your name?

Nobody wakes up one day and decides to be a crackhead. No one drives down the road and suddenly says, "I think I'll go to prison." And no one plans to plummet into shopping addictions, food addictions, or sex addictions, either.

Addictions happen because we have unsatisfied holes in our lives, and we use them to try to satisfy ourselves instead of relying on Jesus. Sadly, addictions and incarceration create a ripple effect of pain that touches more than just the addict or the prisoner.

Conquered or Conquerors

The physical realities of addiction or incarceration are debilitating. These demons rob your freedom, a precious gift from God. They conquer you completely. When you are addicted to a substance or incarcerated, you no longer have control. You are conquered. When someone is conquered, he or she is enslaved. When you are hooked on drugs or alcohol, or when you are bound by the walls of a prison, you have surrendered control of your life.

Perhaps you know someone with one of these two physical limps, or you yourself live under the demonic glare of one or both of these taskmasters. You once thought you had control, but you gave it up to these evil forces. You once could say yes or no. Now your mind and spirit are tormented by the fact that you said yes to the wrong things—to addiction or incarceration. You said yes to being enslaved.

The good news is that it's not too late to reverse course, but you can only do so with God's help. God wants you to know that "all have sinned" (Romans 3:23). Outside of Jesus, all of us are slaves of sin and have said yes to the taskmaster of sin. "My sinful nature [is] a slave to the law of sin" (Romans 7:25). The apostle Paul says that we have been "sold as a slave to sin" (Romans 7:14), so all of us limp. Don't let your taskmaster talk negatively to you and cause you to feel that you are worse than everyone else.

The drugs say, "You cannot break free." The prison walls say, "I have you surrounded." But Romans 6:18 says, "You have been set free from sin and have become slaves to righteousness." You can break free from the walls of sin and serve a kind, good Master: Jesus Christ.

Paul seems to shout out, as if on top of a mountain, "Who shall separate us from the love of Christ? Shall trouble or hardship or persecution or famine or nakedness or danger or sword? . . . In all these things we are more than conquerors through him who loved us" (Romans 8:35, 37).

When your freedom has been ripped from you, your thoughts, your cravings, or your emotions seem out of your control. You cannot move as you once did because a prison has you walled in. If you are the spouse or the child of an addict or an inmate, maybe your spouse's limps have become yours. The enemy may have drawn you into slavery as well.

God says that He is your liberator. Paul said that nothing will separate you from God's love. If you cannot be separated from the love of Christ, then you have hope. That is because Christ alone has conquered all sins. Jesus Christ has overcome this world, and He is calling you into His army. God calls you back to Himself—limps and all. God puts His armor on you, and you can become free to fight for good rather than to surrender to evil.

> GOD CALLS YOU BACK TO HIMSELF—LIMPS AND ALL. GOD PUTS HIS ARMOR ON YOU, AND YOU CAN BECOME FREE TO FIGHT FOR GOOD RATHER THAN TO SURRENDER TO EVIL.

Encourage yourself by paraphrasing Paul's declaration. Fill in the blanks with the addictions you face:

Neither _____ nor _____ shall be able to separate me from the love of God which is in Christ Jesus. In all these things, I am more than a conqueror.

You've probably heard the phrase "Love conquers all." It's true. Only one thing can conquer your taskmaster, and that is the greatest love of all—the love of God in Christ. The Bible says that God is love, and His love breaks addictions and overcomes the pain, stigma, and fallout of sin.

A Love Story

Leslie had limps of addiction and incarceration, even though she was never an actual addict or prisoner herself. Leslie was a college graduate who had always been gainfully employed. She was bright, attractive, and professional. She had always made the right decisions, except in one area.

"I loved thugs," she recently confessed to our church family. Like many "straight-laced" women, she had an inexplicable craving for relationships with wild guys. She looked for love in all the wrong places. She soon became a thug's girlfriend, and that meant adopting a thug's lifestyle. The thug Leslie fell in love with is named Reginald. They eventually married.

There is a happy, hopeful ending to Leslie and Reginald's story, but their life still remains full of limps because of bad past decisions. When they were dating, Reginald was an addict running from the law, and he didn't give up the street life after they married. It didn't help that Leslie kept enabling him. Reginald was arrested so many times that a local bail bonder ran him a line of credit for the bonds he needed to get out of jail.

> IF YOU WANT TO OVERCOME THE EFFECTS OF ADDICTION AND INCARCERATION, THEN YOU MUST UNDERSTAND THE PRINCIPLES OF BEING CONVINCED AND CONNECTED.

The couple endured desperate times. Then, by the grace of God, Leslie and Reginald joined our church. They married and sought to improve their lives. Leslie expected God suddenly to rain down blessings on them, but Reginald's drug addiction and related crime activity continued, and the long-term consequences of these limps were being made manifest.

Eventually, Reginald was arrested and sentenced to 18 months in prison. By this time, the couple had three young children. A terrible cycle began as this new reality impacted their children.

Every Saturday for the next 18 months, Leslie and her children got up early and traveled two hours to visit Reginald in prison. All the while, the children struggled to understand what was happening. Why couldn't they just be like their friends and play outside and watch TV on Saturdays?

Today, Reginald is free from prison and addiction, though he has to remain vigilant so as not to fall back into his old lifestyle. He and Leslie are filled with hope; however, they still encounter consequences from their past. There are remnants that linger, but through Christ they know that they will be overcome.

The limps, however, no longer rule them. That is because they are convinced and connected. If you want to overcome the effects of addiction and incarceration, then you too must understand the principles of being convinced and connected.

Be Convinced

Franklin is a strong man with the chiseled face of a soldier and the body of a boxer. But once upon a time, drugs crushed him. He lost money and a good job, and he went to prison. He lost his first wife and the respect of his children. But after hitting rock bottom, Franklin turned to God; and after a long, painful process, God delivered him.

The first thing Franklin had to do to begin to heal was to surrender. If you limp due to addiction and incarceration, you must surrender, too. You must not let your pride stop you from limping toward Jesus. You must become convinced that submitting to and following Christ is the only way.

Franklin's will had never been broken. He had tried to conquer his limps on his own, but this time he surrendered. "*Surrender* is a hard word for a man. I'm a father, a husband, I got my boys. I'm a man! And you're telling me to give up, God, you're telling me to give up!" But God told Franklin that he had it all wrong. God said to him, "I don't want you to give up, I want you to give in." Franklin did give in, and he has now recovered. He has a new job as a personal fitness trainer, and he is happily married again.

What has baffled Franklin the most since God set his crippled life back on a straight, safe path is the love of God. He just can't understand how God could love an addict who had messed up so badly. Once you surrender to God, once you quit trying to overcome addiction and incarceration's terrible effect on your life, you will be overcome with the awe of God's love for you—in the past, in the present, and in the future.

Franklin recently told our church. "Today, I don't even try to understand God's love any more. God has continued expressing his love to me until I've just accepted it. It's beyond my ability to understand." Through the love of God, Franklin finally became convinced that Christ was strong enough to conquer the effects of his sins and that outside of Jesus, he would be nothing but a slave to sin.

Before I came to the Lord, I was attending the University of Southern Mississippi. The school was right across from a liquor store. It opened at ten in the morning, and I had a class that started at ten. My friend and I would buy alcohol first and take it to class. Later, I realized that I didn't have the power to stop my addiction, but God helped me conquer it.

> ONCE YOU SURRENDER TO GOD, ONCE YOU QUIT TRYING TO OVERCOME ADDICTION AND INCARCERATION'S TERRIBLE EFFECT ON YOUR LIFE, YOU WILL BE OVERCOME WITH THE AWE OF GOD'S LOVE FOR YOU.

The Bible says, "I can do all things through [Christ] who gives me strength," and "my God will meet all your needs according to the riches of his glory in Christ Jesus" (Philippians 4:13, 19). You can do *all* things through Christ, and He will supply *all* of your needs. Paul said that "in *all* of these things we are more than conquerors" (Romans 8:37). This means we have an overwhelming victory.

One songwriter wrote, "There is a fountain filled with blood drawn from Immanuel's veins, and sinners plunged beneath that flood lose all their guilty stains." However, there is a condition attached to these promises: You must be convinced of God's promises.

In Romans 8:38, Paul says, "I am convinced." He was convinced that Christ is the only way to deliverance: "But God demonstrates His own love for us in this: While we were still sinners, Christ died for us" (Romans 5:8). First John 4:9 says, "This is how God showed his love among us: He sent his one and only Son into the world that we might live through him." You have to be convinced that Christ died for you, loves you this very second, and will help you conquer the limps of addiction and incarceration in your life.

What if you fall back into these sins and limps? Sometimes we do. But God's salvation is not based on

> WE DON'T WAKE UP EVERY DAY FEELING, ACTING, OR LOOKING SAVED; BUT WE MUST BE CONVINCED THAT WE ARE. JESUS ALREADY IS, AND WE MUST BE, TOO.

how we feel; it's based on fact. We don't wake up every day feeling, acting, or looking saved; but we must be convinced that we are. Jesus already is, and we must be, too.

In the middle of your addictions or prison cell, you must cry out as the psalmist did: "Do not utterly forsake me" (Psalm 119:8). Then Jesus will say, "Never will I leave you; never will I forsake you" (Hebrews 13:5). He will never forsake you, and nothing can separate Him from you.

Be Connected

The connection you have with Christ is unique, and it can't be broken. No matter what your limp is, it can't break your connection with Christ. Jesus didn't save you to lose you. You are connected to the Source of Life, and He is the Living Water, the Way, the Truth, and the Life.

When Vic got busted for drugs, his father disowned him. The two were no longer connected. Yet, even when his earthly father had abandoned him, his heavenly Father remained connected to him.

This divine connection can change us. John 15:5-8 says that if we remain connected to Christ and He also to us, then we can bear much fruit. That is, we can produce the right kind of things in our own lives and also in the lives of others. This passage goes on to say that if we remain connected to Christ and live by His Word, then whatever we ask in prayer will be done.

When you are convinced and connected, then God will often return to you what you feel unworthy to ask for. That has been the case for Vic. Today, he is clean, and God gave him back his old job. God even restored his relationship with his father, and Vic finally understands the connection he has with Jesus.

If you think you will never beat the physical limps of addiction and incarceration, you are right. You alone never will. But with Jesus you can. He wants you to be restored because He is a God of restoration.

If you feel as if you can never live for Jesus again or that you've blown it as a Christian, don't give up. Instead, connect with Christ. He will hear your prayers to be restored from the limps of addiction and incarceration, and He will deliver you.

EPILOGUE

The Bible provides us with clear evidence that even people of God can have limps, and it is probable that not all of our *limps* will be healed on this side of heaven.

After Jacob wrestled with God, he limped because the socket of his hip had been touched near the tendon (Genesis 32:32). The apostle Paul pleaded with the Lord three times to take away the thorn in his flesh, which was never identified, but it also could be classified as a *limp*. The Lord told Paul that His grace was sufficient and that His power was made perfect in weakness (2 Corinthians 12:7-10). The Bible does not say whether Jacob or Paul were ever healed. As far as we know, both *limped in some way* for the rest of their lives.

The power to keep walking regardless of our *limps* is directly related to our ability to trust in God. In this book, we have seen a wide range of issues that people face over the course of their lives. Nevertheless, they keep pressing.

The reason I describe some of the limps other people have faced is to help you to relate directly or indirectly. I believe in the supernatural power of God to take away all of our limps, but I also know biblically and experientially that God does not always immediately take away every limp that we face. However, He gives us the supernatural power and grace to live with life's limps.

The Lord set an appointment for you to read this book so you would know that He wants to use you for His glory to help others to keep walking. God uses people with limps, and He factored yours in when He gave you your assignment. He was well aware of the days, weeks, months, or years that you would spend in self-pity, anger, and other feelings you may have experienced. Take it from a man who has lived with past limps that have been healed and who currently lives with limps wherein God's grace has proven sufficient.

We all must live with "the already" and "the not yet" when it comes to the issues we face on this side of heaven. Jesus came that we might have life and have it more abundantly (John 10:10), but He never promised we would not have any limps. Yesterday is gone, and tomorrow will be too late; so now is the time to rise up from any consequential despair from our limps. Let us take up our mats and live victoriously through Christ with life's limps.

DWAYNE K. PICKETT MINISTRIES (HOPE NOW)

Key Scripture: Matthew 6:33

Dwayne K. Pickett Ministries: Hope Now Broadcast

Motto: Providing hope for the hopeless

Mission: Our mission is to provide hope for the hopeless. We seek to provide evangelistic empowerment, educational empowerment, and economic empowerment through the systematic teaching and preaching of the Word of God. We believe that through the power of the Holy Spirit and proper discipleship, every person, regardless of his or her background, can live lives that glorify God.

Vision: Transforming men, women, and children to become devoted disciples (true followers) of Jesus Christ in order to build strong families, churches, and communities for the glory of God

Explanation/Philosophy: We believe that in order to effectively transform communities, we must specifically focus on developing men and boys. In no way are we excluding women or girls; however, it is our belief that we must develop and equip strong men to step into their rightful place of being godly leaders of their families, the church, and their communities. Our hearts are extremely burdened with the fact that many girls and boys are growing up without strong godly men in their lives. Undoubtedly, this has created a level of destruction and despair that has fostered a hopeless environment for many, such as an ever-expanding prison population as well as a failing educational system that has caused systemic poverty. We believe that there is hope, that this can be turned around through teaching men (women and children, too) to obey the Word of God.

Ministry Components:

- Missions: foreign and local (orphans, education, boys, etc.)

- Joshua Project: A selective program for men beginning at the age of 16 who desire to enter into a 24-month mentoring relationship with Pastor Pickett.

- Communication: Sermons, books, blogging, social media, etc.

- Media Ministry: TV, radio, live streaming, etc.

- Consulting: Church growth, pastors, business leaders, school administrators, men's discipleship

- Conferences: Retreat center, crusades, men's discipleship, seminars, retreats for men, boys, women, couples, veterans, racial reconciliation, etc.

- Ministry Partners: Regular communication, prayer requests, mentoring, financial support, etc.

- Boys School: 6-12 school that seeks to educate boys from all walks of life

- Fresh Start: Program designed to help men who have been incarcerated as well as those who have supported themselves through illegal activity

CPSIA information can be obtained
at www.ICGtesting.com
Printed in the USA
FFOW03n1947300817
39426FF